Your Love for God

HOW TO LIVE THE FIRST AND GREAT COMMANDMENT TODAY

Elaine Leonard

TRILOGY CHRISTIAN PUBLISHERS

TUSTIN, CA

Trilogy Christian Publishers
A Wholly Owned Subsidiary of Trinity Broadcasting Network
2442 Michelle Drive
Tustin, CA 92780

For information, address Trilogy Christian Publishing

Rights Department, 2442 Michelle Drive, Tustin, Ca 92780.

Trilogy Christian Publishing/ TBN and colophon are trademarks of Trinity Broadcasting Network.

For information about special discounts for bulk purchases, please contact Trilogy Christian Publishing.

Manufactured in the United States of America

10 9 8 7 6 5 4 3 2 1

Library of Congress Cataloging-in-Publication Data is available.
ISBN 978-1-64773-718-4
ISBN 978-1-64773-719-1 (ebook)

Contents

Dedication

To the memory of my parents, Nunzio "Bob" and Angelina Perrotti, who introduced me to Father God and my Savior, Jesus Christ, and daily demonstrated what a life devoted to God looked like through prayer, the Word, worship, and service. I look forward to worshiping Him together again one day in glory.

Acknowledgements

First and foremost, I want to thank God for His ever-present love for me. Without Him I would have nothing to give or to write about. He is my everything. Next, I am so thankful for my amazing husband Larry, for his constant support and encouragement. His wisdom and lightheartedness were the perfect combination for me on this journey. I am also grateful to my daughters and their husbands, Leslie and Chris Abshier and Deborah and Johannes Karlsen, and to my son Luke, for their insightful comments. They added much to my understanding in their areas of strength about producing a work like this. I want to say thank you as well to many of my friends and family who partnered with me in prayer, support, and encouragement, from the beginning to the very end. To name a few: Keith and Judy Gilbert, Rita Fiorentino, Bill and Katrina Dougherty and those at Bread of Life Ministries, Dale Sides, Sandy Ramos, Linda Ray, and Donna Diver—thank you. Lastly, I am so grateful to Mark Mingle, Brad Patton, Kerry Benson, and the amazing team at Trilogy Publishing. Your creativity, uplifting words, and patience through this process have been a blessing. I count it a privilege to work with all of you. Thank you.

Introduction

Loving God is a deep issue of the heart for me. I was introduced to Him at a very young age in my home with a big Bible on the coffee table in the living room, a picture of Jesus and a cross on the wall, and lots of prayers. I would cry every year leading up to Easter as I heard about what Jesus went through for us because He loved us. As I grew up in the church I learned and experienced more about my faith, and my love for God grew.

Yes, I loved Him because He first loved me. My heart was full of affection whenever I thought about God and experienced blessings. However, this love was mostly based on an emotional response to what I was learning and receiving.

It was an eye-opening drive in my car that woke me up to the limits I had on my love for Him. Listening to worship music when I drive is a habit that I enjoy. One day, after joining with a song and singing my love to Him, I sensed the Lord asking, "What are the great commandments?" I quickly and confidently said, "Love God, and love your neighbor." To my surprise, He said, "Look them up." I pulled over to a safe place and opened up the Bible I had in my car. The index in the back helped me to find Mark chapter 12. I read:

And you shall love the Lord your God with all your heart, with all your soul, with all your mind, and with all your strength. This is the first commandment. And the second, like it, is this: You shall love your neighbor as yourself. There is no other commandment greater than these (Mark 12:30-31 NKJV).

I was convicted that I had minimized both commandments, leaving out vital aspects of these very important words of Christ. Realizing that I didn't understand all of what was involved in loving God and loving my neighbor, I decided to pursue this further.

This book is the summation of my pursuit into the first of the two commandments. Since loving God has been a lifetime quest for me, this is where my focus began.

I believe that for anyone who is a lover of God, and for anyone seeking to find Him, this pursuit and focus on the "how" to love Him is an important road to travel sometime in your life. I pray this book will help you along that path.

Love and blessings,
Elaine

The Word of God is Alive!

(You will definitely want to read this.)

When I took my first Bible research class, it changed the way I interacted with the Bible. The Bible, especially the life of Jesus, was always of interest to me, but I have to admit that I read it like any other book. I read it to get information. It was during this class that I realized that the Bible was actually words from God. The men wrote, but God moved through them what to write by way of the Holy Spirit.

Knowing this first of all, that no prophecy of Scripture comes from someone's own interpretation. For no prophecy was ever produced by the will of man, but men spoke from God as they were carried along by the Holy Spirit (2 Peter 1:20-21 ESV).

I also saw that when God speaks, there is power—power to create, power to change, and power to heal.

And God said, "Let there be light," and there was light (Genesis 1:3 ESV).

By the word of the Lord the heavens were made, and all the host of them by the breath of His mouth (Psalm 33:6 NKJV).

We see by reading Genesis chapter 1 that God created the earth and everything in it by His spoken words. Also, when Jesus came to earth, He did the same.

He said to the man who was paralyzed—"I say to you, rise, pick up your bed and go home." And immediately he rose up before them and picked up what he had been lying on and went home, glorifying God (Luke 5:24b-25 ESV).

Jesus spoke of a man having great faith because he knew that Jesus only had to speak for his servant to be changed by His words, even though spoken from afar.

"But say the word, and let my servant be healed." When Jesus heard these things, he marveled at him, and… said, "I tell you, not even in Israel have I found such faith." And when those who had been sent returned to the house, they found the servant well (Luke 7:7b, 9-10 ESV).

God doesn't change. His words still carry power.

For the word of God is living and powerful, and sharper than any two-edged sword, piercing even to the division of soul and spirit, and of joints and marrow, and is a discerner of the thoughts and intents of the heart (Hebrews 4:12 NKJV).

Jesus used the spoken words of Scripture to fight off Satan when tempted by him. *Then Jesus was led up by the Spirit into the wilderness to be tempted by the devil. And when He had fasted forty days and forty nights, afterward He was hungry. Now when the tempter came to Him, he said, "If You are the Son of God, command that these stones become bread." But He answered and said, "It is written, 'Man shall not live by bread alone, but by every word that proceeds from the mouth of God'"* (Matthew 4:1-4 NKJV).

Jesus knew that we are to live from every word that comes from God. In this temptation, Satan questioned Jesus' identity by saying, "If you are the Son of God." Jesus spoke out a truth of the Bible instead of considering what Satan said. We can do the same—speak truths from the Bible—during this kind of temptation, and many other kinds of attacks.

God tells us that we are in warfare against evil, so we must put on His armor. One of those pieces to use is the sword of the Spirit, which is God's Word.

Put on the whole armor of God, that you may be able to stand against the wiles of the devil. For we do not wrestle against flesh and blood, but against principalities, against powers, against the rulers of the darkness of this age, against spiritual hosts of wickedness in the heavenly places. Therefore take up the whole armor of God, that you may be able to withstand in the evil day, and having done all, to stand. Stand therefore... And take... the sword of the Spirit, which is the word of God (Ephesians 6:11-14a,17b NKJV).

I did not use Scripture this way for years but realized I needed to. I wanted to be like the man that Jesus said had great faith. Believing that God's words have power and speaking them into circumstances of life became my goal.

One night I was very sick. I was running a fever and had an intense sore throat. It was so bad that I thought I needed to go to the doctor to probably get an antibiotic, but I decided to read my Bible for twenty-four hours first and believe that what I was reading could heal me. I would fall asleep in the middle of reading, but I kept pushing myself to even speak it out whenever I was awake. I asked God to help me believe, and after about ten hours I woke up and was totally healed! *The words that I speak to you are spirit, and they are life* (John 6:63b NKJV).

Think about it. If it is words—spoken or read—about Jesus that give people the power to get saved and have eternal life, then of course, the Word of God is life-giving and powerful!

Receive with meekness the implanted word, which is able to save your souls (James 1:21b ESV).

His Word gives us the power to change. I have seen many people's lives impacted, healed, and changed for the better because God touched them through His awesome Word.

One time when I was attending a twelve-session Bible teaching series, there was a young man coming who had mental issues. I sat next to him and watched him pick the scabs off his skin and eat them while talking to himself and looking all around the room while the pastor was teaching. I thought, *He is not getting a thing out of this*, but I was wrong. As the sessions went on, I noticed he was calming down. He stopped picking at his skin and appeared to be listening. Then he started looking at a Bible and even talked to me about some of the lessons. When I looked in his eyes, they seemed to have changed color from dark brown to blue, and his skin was now healed and soft like a child's. His mind became whole, and he even got a job. No one had laid hands on him or prayed for him, but this man was totally healed by just listening to the Word of God. *He sent his word, and healed them, and delivered them from their destructions* (Psalm 107:20 KJV) still triumphs in my heart.

God's words have power, and now He's given them to us to do the same.

And Jesus came and spoke to them, saying, "All authority has been given to Me in heaven and on earth. Go therefore and make disciples of all the nations, baptizing them in the name of the Father and of the Son and of the Holy Spirit, teaching them to observe all things that I have commanded you; and lo, I am with you always, even to the end of the age." Amen (Matthew 28:18-20 NKJV).

You will see many Scripture verses woven throughout the writing in this book. This is because I believe in the life-giving power of God's Word. Your life can be changed by reading His words, so take the time to read and ponder them.

So then faith comes by hearing, and hearing by the word of God (Romans 10:17 NKJV).

If you abide in My word, you are My disciples indeed. And you shall know the truth, and the truth shall make you free (John 8:31b-32 NKJV).

Believe with me for His truth to set you free to walk in the liberty that Christ Jesus died for you to have. Then you can be all God created you to be, and then love Him.

The entrance of Your words gives light; it gives understanding to the simple (Psalm 119:130 NKJV).

Your word I have hidden in my heart, that I might not sin against You (Psalm 119:11 NKJV).

This is my comfort in my affliction, for Your word has given me life (Psalm 119:50 ESV).

Your word is a lamp to my feet and a light to my path (Psalm 119:105 ESV).

Your word is very pure; therefore Your servant loves it (Psalm 119:140 NKJV).

CHAPTER 1

We Love Him Because He First Loved Us

God... wants... your... love. Think about that. The Creator of the heavens and the earth, the Almighty One, the all-wise, all-knowing, omnipresent God, who is love, desires your unique love.

1 Corinthians 12:14-18 (KJV) says, *For the body is not one member, but many. If the foot shall say, Because I am not the hand, I am not of the body; is it therefore not of the body? And if the ear shall say, Because I am not the eye, I am not of the body; is it therefore not of the body? If the whole body were an eye, where were the hearing? If the whole were hearing, where were the smelling? But now hath God set the members every one of them in the body, as it hath pleased him.*

From this we understand that God made each of us uniquely different—but necessary—members of the Body of Christ. No one is alike, but everyone is important. In Psalm 139:14a (KJV) we read, *I will praise thee; for I am fearfully and wonderfully made; marvelous are your works.*

Yes, each one of us is an amazing, unique individual that God has created. Therefore, He cannot receive the kind of love that you would give Him from anyone else but you. He will also not receive the way you would love Him from anyone else but you. You are the only one who can love Him in your unique and wonderful way, so God wants *your* love.

In any relationship, someone initiates the communication, but the other person must respond if the relationship is going to continue. How far and how deep the union goes is up to both parties. If someone is pouring out their heart, but the recipient only lets them in so far by staying busy and distant to avoid being hurt, then their relationship will stay on the surface.

God initiated a relationship with you and me. He poured out His whole self. He sent the one He loved, Jesus, from heaven to the earth. Why would the Father give up His Son to a life on earth, ending in a painful and sorrowful death? He did it because He loves you. The Good News Translation in 1 John 4:9 says, *And God showed his love for us by sending his only Son into the world, so that we might have life through him.* That is good news! Romans 5:8 (NKJV) says it this way: *But God demonstrates His own love toward us, in that while we were still sinners, Christ died for us.* Even in your imperfect state, the truth is that God loves you so much that He sent Jesus to die for you. How much does He love you? He loves you the same as He loves Jesus. How do I know that? Jesus prayed this in John 17:23b (NKJV): *That the world may know that You have sent Me, and have loved them as You have loved Me.* As the Father loves Jesus, that's how much He loves you! Yes, He loves you that much!

God welcomes you with open arms to come to Him so He can give you His best. You can see this in the parable of the Prodigal Son that Jesus taught in Luke 15, verses 11-24 (NKJV).

> *Then He said: "A certain man had two sons. And the younger of them said to his father, 'Father, give me the portion of goods that falls to me.' So he divided to them his livelihood. And not many days after, the younger son gathered all together, journeyed to a far country, and there wasted his possessions with prodigal living. But when he had spent all, there arose a severe famine in that land, and he began to be in want. Then he went and joined himself to a citizen of that country, and he sent him into his fields to feed swine. And he would*

gladly have filled his stomach with the pods that the swine ate, and no one gave him anything. But when he came to himself, he said, 'How many of my father's hired servants have bread enough and to spare, and I perish with hunger! I will arise and go to my father, and will say to him, "Father, I have sinned against heaven and before you, and I am no longer worthy to be called your son. Make me like one of your hired servants."' And he arose and came to his father. But when he was still a great way off, his father saw him and had compassion, and ran and fell on his neck and kissed him. And the son said to him, 'Father, I have sinned against heaven and in your sight, and am no longer worthy to be called your son.' But the father said to his servants, 'Bring out the best robe and put it on him, and put a ring on his hand and sandals on his feet. And bring the fatted calf here and kill it, and let us eat and be merry; for this my son was dead and is alive again; he was lost and is found.' And they began to be merry."

The father's love in this parable was extravagant, giving his best to his wayward son. Our heavenly Father's love is the same toward us. His love far surpasses the kind of love we have experienced on earth. His love is unselfish. It is not determined by our behavior, our appearance, or our response. It is a pure love based on who He is, not on who we are. 1 John 4:8b (ESV) states that *God is love*, and 1 John 1:5b (ESV) says, *God is light, and in Him is no darkness at all.* Isn't this the good and perfect love we've all been craving and needing?

1 Corinthians 13 is the chapter in the Bible that tells of the attributes of love. If God is love, then God is all of those attributes listed in verses 4 through 8. I have inserted the word "God" in place of "love" in these verses.

God *is patient and is kind;* God *doesn't envy.* God *doesn't brag, is not proud, doesn't behave inappropriately, doesn't seek* His *own way, is not provoked, takes no account of evil; doesn't rejoice in unrighteousness, but rejoices with the truth;* He *bears all things, believes all things, hopes all things, and endures all things.* God *never fails* (WEB).

This is who God is, and Jesus' life shows us how much He loves. Jesus said in John 5:19b (NKJV), *The Son can do nothing of Himself, but what He sees the Father do; for whatever He does, the Son also does in like manner.* Jesus only said and did what He saw the Father saying and doing.

What was the Father doing when Jesus hugged the leper? What was the Father saying when Jesus told the prostitute she was forgiven? What was the Father doing when Jesus raised the little girl from the dead? What was the Father saying when Jesus said to the crippled man, "Arise, take up your bed, and walk"? The Father was doing and saying all these things. Jesus carried out these and many more miracles of love, because He saw and heard the Father do them.

This kind of love can only be found in God.

He loves you with an everlasting love.

He is for you, not against you.

He has wonderful plans for you.

He sets you free.

He gives you a life in eternity and much, much more.

It's hard to imagine the depth of this kind of love being poured out to us. However, it's the truth. That's the love God has for us, and He wants us to know and experience it every day of our lives.

That Christ may dwell in your hearts through faith; that you, being rooted and grounded in love, may be able to comprehend with all the saints what is the width and length and depth and height—to know the love of Christ which passes knowledge; that you may be filled with all the fullness of God (Ephesians 3:17-19 NKJV).

Wow! This Scripture says that love has four dimensions and is higher than anything we know. That's the greatness of God's love for us. How do we respond to that? Our response to His love is recorded in 1 John 4:19

(KJV): *We love Him, because He first loved us.* When some-one gives you so much, doesn't it move you to want to love them back? We can! Then we will receive and ex-perience even more of His love, which will cause us to want to love Him even more. This cycle of love can con-tinue into eternity.

But some ask, how do we love someone whom we cannot see or touch?

Jesus instructs us in Mark 12:28-30 (NKJV), *Then one of the scribes came, and having heard them reasoning togeth-er, perceiving that He had answered them well, asked Him, "Which is the first commandment of all?"*

Jesus answered him, "The first of all the commandments is: 'Hear, O Israel, the Lord our God, the Lord is one. And you shall love the Lord your God with all your heart, with all your soul, with all your mind, and with all your strength.' This is the first commandment."

In Matthew 22:38 (KJV), Jesus says, *This is the first and great commandment.*

He tells us that to love God is the first and greatest truth to live by. Of all the spiritual disciplines in our lives here on earth, loving God is *first*. First means noth-ing else comes before it. *Nothing!*

Let's stop and evaluate for a minute—is loving God really the first priority of your heart? Is loving God taking first place in your soul? Is loving God the absolute first focus of your mind? Is loving God first in your physical life? What do I need to lay aside or put lower in my priorities to move God up to that first spot in my life? If Jesus says it is not only the first, but the *great* commandment, what am I missing by not doing this?

If I told you I read a great book or watched a great movie, you would probably want to know about it. If you told me you ate a great meal last night, I would want to know what it was and where you got it, or what's the recipe. The word *great* exemplifies a quality that usually gets our attention. Now think about who said that it was great. That person was Jesus, who is the truth (John 14:6). This should grab our attention even more, because He is not exaggerating at all!

In Mark 12:30, Jesus revealed that we can love God with four different parts of ourselves: our heart, our soul, our mind, and our strength. It's not enough to just *think* that you love Him, or to have an emotional attachment to Him. Christ makes it clear that we are to love Him from all four areas of ourselves.

He doesn't stop there, though. Not only are we to love God with each part, but with "all" of each one: our heart, our soul, our mind, and our strength. "All" means leaving nothing out, the whole thing, every single bit.

He specifically uses the phrase "with all of your" before each of these four areas.

Jesus tells you to love God:

With all of your heart,

With all of your soul,

With all of your mind, and

With all of your strength.

By repeating the phrase "with all of your" each time, He is emphasizing that we are to hold nothing back in the area of our heart, in the area of our soul, in the area of our mind, and in the area of our strength. Holding nothing back in each area will look different for me than for you, because "your" makes it unique to each person. "All" conveys the entirety of who we are, and "your" conveys that it belongs to you and is up to you. How do we each do that?

We know that Jesus wouldn't tell us to do something we weren't able to do.

God is not man, that he should lie, or a son of man, that he should change his mind. Has he said, and will he not do it? Or has he spoken, and will he not fulfill it? (Numbers 23:19 ESV).

If we are to love Him with all of each part of us, let us ask, seek, and knock, knowing that God will help us to love Him more.

Ask, and it will be given to you; seek, and you will find; knock, and it will be opened to you. For everyone who asks receives, and the one who seeks finds, and to the one who knocks it will be opened (Matthew 7:7-8 ESV).

Yes, God wants your love. How do you know that? A commandment is an instruction, given by a person who wants the receiver to do it. God wants you to love Him. He wants you to give Him all of your love, so let's learn how.

In the chapters that follow, we will individually look at heart, soul, mind, and strength. We will give attention to things that get in the way in each area. Then we will discover how we can grow in ways to give our love to God with all of our heart, and all of our soul, as well as all of our mind and all of our strength. This will help us to fulfill what Jesus said was the *first* and *great* commandment.

You shall love the Lord your God with all your heart, with all your soul, with all your strength, and with all your mind (Luke 10:27 NKJV).

CHAPTER 2

Love God with ALL YOUR HEART

God longs for your heart. No, He doesn't just want "the organ in your chest that sends the blood around your body,"[1] but He desires "the place within a person where feelings or emotions are considered to come from."[2]

You have the power to set your love, your heart, on God. You can give Him some of it or all of it; it's up to you. He would not be a God of love if He forced Himself on us or made us love Him. Love, by its very nature, is voluntary. If someone tells you they love you, you do not—whether through obligation, coercion, or guilt—have to love them back. It is 100% your freewill choice to decide whether you want to give them your heart or not. Otherwise, it is not real love.

If a person shows you that they love you by telling you, being loving and kind, taking care of you, giving you gifts, spending time with you, and many other demonstrations of their affection, you may start loving them back. It can be immediate, but usually love is something that grows. As you get to know someone and see how they are—their nature, so to speak—you can either be more or less attracted to them. Your desire to be with them may increase, and your emotions toward them may grow. The happiness you start feeling may cause you to want more, so you spend even more time talking and being together. Affectionate touch and more intimate topics of discussion may become part of your relationship. Whether there is joy, excitement, nervousness, or a myriad of other feelings, your emotions are definitely involved at this point. The timing it takes for a person to step into love for another is really up to them. For some, it takes a long time. For others, it can be relatively fast, but it is a personal determination of each human being. To give our heart to someone is always our unique choice, in our unique timing.

God wouldn't have it any other way. He created us in His image.

So God created man in his own image, in the image of God he created him; male and female he created them (Genesis 1:27 ESV).

Our God is not an apathetic God, showing little or no emotion. He is a God of passion, with emotions and affections, and His design is for us to have them too. However, His emotions come from His holiness, so in them He never sins. We, on the other hand, are learning how to do that.

For I am the Lord who brought you up out of the land of Egypt to be your God. You shall therefore be holy, for I am holy (Leviticus 11:45 ESV).

Be angry and do not sin; do not let the sun go down on your anger (Ephesians 4:26 ESV).

When I was growing up, I learned that God was a safe place to go with my emotions. When I was highly emotional, if I shared it with some family or friends they would give me logical solutions, trying to fix what I was feeling. Sometimes people would disregard what I was feeling, and still other times people would get highly emotional with me, either in opposition or in agreement. Now don't get me wrong, sometimes these responses were appropriate, but other times they weren't, or I wasn't ready to receive them. I finally tried going for a walk or to my room, saying and pouring out whatever I was feeling to God. It worked! I realized that God had big enough shoulders to handle whatever emotions I was dealing with, accepted me no matter what I was going through, and could comfort or direct me as needed. Sometimes I would feel better after talking with Him alone, and other times He would inspire me as to whom I could talk to about what was bothering me. Either way, God understood the best way to deal with my emotions each time. That's how I learned to go to Him first.

One emotional time in my life I was walking up and down our long driveway, pouring out my thoughts and emotions to Him. All of a sudden, a baby bird landed right in front of me as a squirrel scurried up to get it. I quickly scared it away to protect the little bird. I knew in that moment that God was showing me that He does the same for me. He understood how I felt in that moment and sent me an answer that calmed my fear. What a shelter, what a Father, what a friend!

King David, in the Old Testament, also went to God with his myriad of emotions.

I am weary with my moaning; every night I flood my bed with tears; I drench my couch with my weeping. My eye wastes away because of grief; it grows weak because of all my foes (Psalm 6:6-7 ESV).

You, Lord, hear the desire of the afflicted; you encourage them, and you listen to their cry (Psalm 10:17 NIV).

We see Jesus pouring out His feelings to the Father as well.

Then Jesus came with them to a place called Gethsemane, and said to the disciples, "Sit here while I go and pray over there." And He took with Him Peter and the two sons of Zebedee, and He began to be sorrowful and deeply distressed. Then He said to them, "My soul is exceedingly sorrowful, even to death. Stay here and watch with Me." He went a little farther and fell on His face, and prayed, saying, "O My Father, if it is possible, let this cup pass from Me; nevertheless, not as I will, but as You will" (Matthew 26:36-39 NKJV).

Hebrews 4:15 (NIV) tells us that Jesus empathizes with us. *For we do not have a high priest who is unable to empathize with our weaknesses, but we have one who has been tempted in every way, just as we are—yet he did not sin.*

The Oxford Dictionary states that *empathy* means "to understand and share the feelings of another."[3] Jesus is that kind of Savior and friend, experiencing emotions like us. Therefore, He certainly is a safe place to show and share what's in our hearts.

The Lord also will be a refuge for the oppressed, a refuge in times of trouble. And those who know Your name will put their trust in You; for You, Lord, have not forsaken those who seek You (Psalm 9:9-10 NKJV).

Your heart is yours. It's part of who you are, unique and wonderful, the way God created you. What you feel, how you process those feelings, and how you respond can be a combination of your unique creative design and your environmental influences. What I mean is that you may not naturally be an extremely emotional person, but a specific incident may occur in your life that sparks an intense emotion in you. Or you may be a very sensitive person by nature, born to feel deeply and then respond in an emotional way. Then as you grew up, you faced some difficult times and situations, so those responses and emotions could have either intensified or been squelched, depending on the people you were with and the choices you internally made. These are just a couple of examples of how our hearts can change as we live in this world and grow. Life can be hard at times, and our reactions to those tough encounters can cause us to protect our hearts, hold back, and even shut down parts of ourselves to others. Therefore, one thing you can do to love with your whole heart is to open up parts of your heart that may have been hurt or shut down.

The heart I was living from years ago is not the same as the one I am living from today. My family will tell you that I am a crier. I cry at movies, when others are hurting, when I worship, and just about any time something touches me. However, early in my life I chose not to show that side. Sarcasm and humor were common tactics where I grew up. To avoid being the target, I shut down, deflected, or pretended things didn't bother me. Of course, this caused even more hurt and pain from holding things in. Outwardly I was friendly and nice, but if you got close you might have seen a wounded, defensive side.

For the Lord sees not as man sees: man looks on the outward appearance, but the Lord looks on the heart (1 Samuel 16:7b ESV).

However, God is faithful, and He started helping me to change. One day in prayer, I believe the Holy Spirit showed me that the walls I had built up to protect my heart were also keeping good things out that God wanted me to receive. Crying, I asked Him to help me tear them down, and step-by-step He has, and still is. I can now live out of the heart I believe God designed for me.

Forgiveness

One of the first and biggest bricks I had to deal with in the wall around my heart was unforgiveness. I was angry and hurt, and my heart was covered up, not willing to be vulnerable and open again. I had trusted and was let down. Can you relate? We all can, to various degrees. Whether it was family, friends, people we work with, those in church, or complete strangers, we have all been let down, hurt, or used. It's not right, and it's not fair, but our Lord gave us an undeniable example of forgiveness when He was hanging on the cross. After He was rejected, betrayed, humiliated, abandoned, mocked, tortured, abused, and crucified, He said in Luke 23:34 (KJV), *Father, forgive them; for they know not what they do.*

I believe that everyone who has sinned against you and me—those who have hurt us, whether in big ways or small—in some way did not know what they were doing in their heart of hearts. Yes, some made a deliberate decision but made it out of their own hurt, deception, suffering, generational curses, or sins. They did not have the full understanding of what they were doing. This does not excuse them for their actions. We all are accountable for what we say and do.

Each of us will give an account of himself to God. Therefore let us not pass judgment on one another any longer, but rather decide never to put a stumbling block or hindrance in the way of a brother (Romans 14:12-13 ESV).

Just as the people who hurt us are accountable for their words or actions, we are also accountable for how we judge them and hold it against them. However, when you release them through forgiveness, you release yourself. You are the one set free. The Mayo Clinic says, "Forgiveness can lead to: healthier relationships, greater spiritual and psychological well-being, less anxiety, stress, and hostility, lower blood pressure, fewer symptoms of depression, stronger immune system, improved heart health, and higher self-esteem."[4] Do you want to reap the benefits of forgiving? Isn't it time for you to have that part of your heart back?

When I was fifteen years old, I was in a car accident. Two girlfriends and I were walking to get food when some friends pulled up. They were driving to do the same thing so they invited us to go with them. I jumped in the front seat, and they got in the back. As we crossed a divided highway, the trees in the median were blocking our view of a car coming. Out of the corner of my eye I saw the car crash into the side of us. I was thrown forward into the dashboard and broke my jaw, cracked my ribs, and had whiplash. It was a very traumatic incident in my life at the time.

Many years later, at a conference, I was listening to a teaching on forgiveness and the pastor asked anyone that had been in a car accident to stand up. He asked if we had forgiven the driver. I had never even thought about doing that, because it was an accident, not intentional. He led us in a simple prayer to speak out loud: "I forgive (name of the driver). He owes me nothing." As I did that, I heard and felt a pop in the back of my neck. For over twenty-five years I'd have pain in that exact spot when I woke up in the morning. Also, if I rolled over in the middle of the night and ended up on my stomach, I would not be able to turn my head at all. My husband would then have to come and rub my neck to loosen those muscles. The following morning after the meeting, when I woke up, I was lying on my stomach. I expected pain and called out to my husband to help me. Before he got there I turned my head, and all of a sudden I realized that I could move my head from side to side without any pain. The muscles in my neck had responded to the forgiveness I had released the night before, and I have been free from that pain ever since.

Is there a part of you that is knotted up or in pain because of the unforgiveness you are carrying? Forgiveness is a decision, not a feeling. The feelings of hurt may still be there, but you can decide to forgive and let the person go anyway. The person you need to forgive may even be you, but Jesus' suffering is bigger than any offense done to you or by you. Do not let His suffering go to waste. Ask Him to help you. You may have to forgive someone more than once as the Holy Spirit reminds you of things in your past, but as He does, simply speak a statement forgiving the person as many times as it takes, and let God deal with the rest.

Then Peter came to Him and said, "Lord, how often shall my brother sin against me, and I forgive him? Up to seven times?" Jesus said to him, "I do not say to you, up to seven times, but up to seventy times seven" (Matthew 18:21-22 NKJV).

You may even have feelings of unforgiveness toward God. After the car accident I kept asking, "Where were you, God?" I was hurt, offended, and didn't understand why He hadn't protected me, until my dad took me to the junkyard where they had towed the wrecked car. The car, which was hit on the side, was compressed to half its width. My dad asked, "Elaine, looking at the car now, tell me how five people all got out of this alive?" Crying, I admitted, "I don't know. There's no way; there's not even room for all five of us if we were on top of each other." In that moment I knew that somehow, God had protected us. He had saved our lives. God can handle our emotions, even toward Him, so go to Him and pour them out. Like David, you will be a man or woman after His heart.

It is freeing to tear down the walls around your heart by starting to forgive. When you do, you'll have more of your heart back to give. Help your heart to be healed.

Sow forgiveness and freedom, and you will reap forgiveness and freedom back.

Forgive us for our sins, just as we have forgiven those who sinned against us (Matthew 6:12 NCV).

Sow righteousness for yourselves, reap the fruit of unfailing love (Hosea 10:12a NIV).

Wounded Heart

Just because you have forgiven someone doesn't necessarily mean the hurt that was caused goes away at the same time. You may have to deal with this next brick of the wounds in your heart as well.

When the body receives a wound, depending on the degree, it may heal without much assistance. Sometimes it may leave a scar, but other times it may not. However, there are times when a wound needs medical attention. Whether it can be done at home, at a doctor's office, or at a hospital depends on the severity.

I believe wounds of the heart are the same way. There are times when, as a person grows—especially if they have a relationship with the Lord—their heart wounds heal. However, sometimes we may need others to help us. As a child goes to a parent to clean a physical wound, we can go to another in our family or the extended family of God for assistance.

Again I say to you that if two of you agree on earth concerning anything that they ask, it will be done for them by My Father in heaven (Matthew 18:19 NKJV).

There may be times when it would be helpful to go to a pastor or counselor to talk and to receive wise counsel to help with healing. Also, going to elders or ministers for prayer can bring healing results as well.

Are any among you suffering? They should pray. Are any cheerful? They should sing songs of praise. Are any among you sick? They should call for the elders of the church and have them pray over them, anointing them with oil in the name of the Lord. The prayer of faith will save the sick, and the Lord will raise them up; and anyone who has committed sins will be forgiven. Therefore confess your sins to one another, and pray for one another, so that you may be healed. The prayer of the righteous is powerful and effective (James 5:13-16 NRSV).

The word sick in this verse means "weak, feeble, without strength."[5] This is not only in the category of the physical, but can be about our heart, mind, or soul as well. We all need prayer at times, and God states that it is good to ask for help.

People and circumstances are unique, but the healing of your wounded heart is important to our loving

Father. He sent His Son Jesus Christ to forgive your sins, but also for your healing.

At the Passover meal before His death, Jesus exemplified this through the bread and wine. *For I received from the Lord that which I also delivered to you: that the Lord Jesus on the same night in which He was betrayed took bread; and when He had given thanks, He broke it and said, "Take, eat; this is My body which is broken for you; do this in remembrance of Me." In the same manner He also took the cup after supper, saying, "This cup is the new covenant in My blood. This do, as often as you drink it, in remembrance of Me"* (1 Corinthians 11:23-25 NKJV).

What the church calls communion today is an act of remembrance for what Jesus did and accomplished for us. The wine or juice in communion represents His blood, which He bled for the forgiveness of our sins. The bread or cracker in communion represents His body that was broken and tortured for our healing. That healing is for all aspects: heart, soul, mind, and body.

The Spirit of the Lord is upon Me, because He has anointed Me to preach the gospel to the poor; He has sent Me to heal the brokenhearted, to proclaim liberty to the captives and recovery of sight to the blind, to set at liberty those who are oppressed, to proclaim the acceptable year of the Lord (Luke 4:18-19 NKJV).

Dr. Dale M. Sides, in his book *Perfect Redemption*, explains each way that Jesus bled, and what it stands for. Here is his explanation about Jesus bleeding out of His side:

> "When the Bible says that the soldier pierced Jesus' side, the Greek word for *side* is *pleura*. That is the name of the cavity in the chest which contains the heart. For many years, I wondered where the water came from in Jesus' side; then I realized that His ribs were pierced, and the spear went into His heart. Out of his heart came water and blood.

> "The water came from the pericardial sac that surrounds the heart. It is filled with water and serum, and acts as a shock absorber to protect the heart from injury... He bled out of His heart so that yours could be healed."[6]

Your heart is a priority to the Father, so He sent Jesus, His Son, to heal your heart and mine from the brokenness and hurts we have and will endure. You don't have to live with it; you don't have to go through it alone.

He sent the Holy Spirit, who is called the Comforter for a reason. He is with you and understands. He is in you to relieve you of your burdens, to carry your hurts and pains away, and to give you hope and assurance. He helps you and fills you with God's love and acceptance.

I love sitting with a comforter around me—yes, most of the year. My husband and I have different body thermostats, so for me our home is usually on the cool side. The comforter therefore keeps me warm, but also helps me to relax and rest. I feel secure and safe with it around me. The weight reminds me that I am not alone. It may only be a physical representation, but it is a great reminder of the Father's love, the Son's protection, and the Holy Spirit's comfort to me. They never leave me nor forsake me (Hebrews 13:5). They are my constant companions, and that brings joy to my heart.

And I will pray the Father, and he shall give you another Comforter, that he may abide with you forever (John 14:16 KJV).

Hardheartedness

Another brick I had to take out of the wall around my heart was hardheartedness. Hardheartedness can show up in a person being cold, shut down, stubborn, or rebellious, to name a few common responses. When someone's heart is hard, it is difficult for others to get close to them. They won't share anything that would make them vulnerable. They are guarded. They may help others but limit others helping them. Hardheartedness is a defense mechanism around a person's heart to protect them. It's usually an automatic response to a time when the person was young and wounded. As that person grows, the hard responses can be subtle and not even realized at first, but as they mature it will show up in their closest relationships. Others may point it out, pull back from them, or fight with them about it. These characteristics may continue developing into bitterness, resentment, and wrath, causing distrust. Soon, this person may find him or herself feeling attacked, isolated, and alone.

Hardheartedness is a response of the old nature of man, rooted in separation from God.

Among whom we all once lived in the passions of our flesh, carrying out the desires of the body and the mind, and were by nature children of wrath, like the rest of mankind (Ephesians 2:3 ESV).

Once a person turns to God, though, he or she has the help needed to open up his or her heart again.

If you confess with your mouth that Jesus is Lord and believe in your heart that God raised him from the dead, you will be saved (Romans 10:9 ESV).

Therefore if any man be in Christ, he is a new creature: old things are passed away; behold, all things are become new (2 Corinthians 5:17 KJV).

God, our source of help, the source of love, is with you, ready to help when you ask. It is your choice to ask, though. Open up your heart to Him and let Him heal you.

For he is our God, and we are the people of his pasture, and the sheep of his hand. Today, if you hear his voice, do not harden your hearts (Psalm 95:7-8a ESV).

I will give you a new heart and put a new spirit within you; I will take the heart of stone out of your flesh and give you a heart of flesh. I will put My Spirit within you and cause you to walk in My statutes, and you will keep My judgments and do them (Ezekiel 36:26-27 NKJV).

God will remove any hardness in our hearts and give us a new heart, but it is our responsibility to steward it and not harden it again.

Keep thy heart with all diligence; for out of it are the issues of life (Proverbs 4:23 KJV).

When you "keep" something you are responsible for it, to watch over it and make sure it is safe. When you keep or tend a garden, you fertilize and water the seeds and good crops, but you also pull out the weeds and kill the bugs that are destroying the good. Keeping your heart is the same way—protecting the good and getting rid of the bad, like keeping your affections on things of God and guarding your heart from being defiled by sin.

Set your affection on things above, not on things on the earth (Colossians 3:2 KJV).

Doing it with diligence means "giving careful and persistent work or effort," according to the *Oxford Dictionary.*[7] I learned quickly that if I didn't water my garden at least every other day, the plants would start to get weak and wither. Also, if I didn't pull the weeds every week, they would spread and overtake the good plants. I had to be faithful and put in persistent work to reap the benefits of hearty and plentiful vegetables. If I did, there were enough vegetables for my family, as well as plenty to give to friends and neighbors. It is the same way with paying attention to the condition of our hearts. We must be consistent to water the good and pull out the bad, so the result can be a life that produces good fruit, is filled with healthy relationships, and gives glory to God. Then we can carry out the First and Great Commandment to love God with all of our hearts.

I encourage you to pray with me: Lord, I turn to You and confess that You are my Lord and Savior. Forgive me for my sins and for shutting my heart off to You and others. Help me to forgive myself and others, trust again, and open up my heart. Touch me and heal any wounds or hurts, giving me a heart that receives Your love and acceptance and then gives it to others. Just as You were resurrected, so I can receive newness in all areas of my life, like my emotions. I ask You, Father, to remove any stony places of my heart and give me a heart of flesh, so I can walk in Your ways and love You with *all* my heart. Help me to steward my heart well, and, Holy Spirit, comfort and guide me in the truth. I thank You and praise You, in Jesus' holy name, amen.

T.R.U.S.T.

One of the issues of life is trust. When your heart doesn't trust, it holds back. However, when your heart trusts, then you are free—free to move forward, free to give, free to share, free to be 100% present, free to expect good things, and so much more. What is trust? Trust is a confident expectation of good.

There's an acronym that I always refer to whenever I think or talk about trust.

T.R.U.S.T. – Totally Rely Upon Spiritual Truth

T – TOTALLY: that demonstrates trust by its completeness.

R – RELY: that demonstrates trust because you let go and depend on something.

U – UPON: that demonstrates trust because you go up to get on.

S – SPIRITUAL: that demonstrates trust because God is Spirit, and the things of the Spirit are not temporary but eternal.

T – TRUTH: that demonstrates trust because you can depend on and have confidence in the truth, who is Jesus.

Whenever I think of this acronym, I usually picture a person looking forward who lets go of doubt or fear and falls straight back, letting him or herself be caught by the Lord. We have a good God whose eyes are always on us. He knows our coming and going, so He is there to catch us in His strong, loving arms when we fall. We can depend on Him to not let us go. We can rely on Him.

My favorite part of this acronym is the word *rely*. It has a wonderful meaning to consider. When you lie down, your feet are no longer holding you up and supporting you. You have gotten "off of your feet" to let something else, like a bed, support you. When you *rely* on God, you get off of your own feet, your own ability, your own ways of thinking and acting, and let Him support you instead. The prefix "re" means "again," like in the words *rerun, recharge,* and *reuse.* They mean to run again, charge again, and use again. When you "re-ly," you lie down again. You fall back, take the weight off of yourself, and let the Father support you instead. You can do this again and again. Get the pressure or weight off of yourself, and let Him catch and hold you up.

When I am in a struggle, I remind myself to go lie down. It helps me to let go of my own ways and to rest in Him. Then I think about the Lord and ask Him to remind me of a truth from His Word that I can hold on to and believe in this situation. I stop depending on myself and trust that God is able to carry me through, hold me up, and keep me safe and secure.

During one of my pregnancies, I was put on bedrest for the last six weeks. As I lay in bed, praying and listening to an audio version of the Bible week after week, my trust in the Lord grew. I realized that He was holding me and my baby, and that we were safe in His care. My precious daughter was born, and we were both fine.

The Lord is my strength and my shield; my heart trusts in him, and he helps me. My heart leaps for joy, and with my song I praise him (Psalm 28:7 NIV).

Trust in Him at all times, you people; pour out your heart before Him; God is a refuge for us (Psalm 62:8 NKJV).

My heart can trust in Him.

Pour Out Your Heart

Now that you have forgiven whoever came to your mind, and have asked the Lord to heal your heart from pain and hardness so you can trust again, you can give Him more of your heart. It's your freewill choice to love Him, to give Him your affections, your passion, your trust, and your emotions. Yes, all of them—not just your "happy" ones, but whatever is in your heart.

Luke tells us in his gospel of a time when Jesus sat down to eat at a Pharisee's house. A woman of the city, who was a sinner, came in and stood at his feet, weeping. She began to wash his feet with her tears, and then wiped them with her hair while kissing his feet. She had an alabaster box of ointment, which she then used to anoint his feet.

When the Pharisee saw this, he thought, *If this man were a prophet, he would have known who and what sort of woman this is who is touching him, for she is a sinner* (Luke 7:39 ESV).

In Luke 7:41-50 (ESV), it's recorded what Jesus told the Pharisee Simon in response:

"A certain moneylender had two debtors. One owed five hundred denarii, and the other fifty. When they could not pay, he cancelled the debt of both. Now which of them will love him more?" Simon answered, "The one, I suppose, for whom he cancelled the larger debt." And he said to him, "You have judged rightly." Then turning toward the woman he said to Simon, "Do you see this woman? I entered your house; you gave me no water for my feet, but she has wet my feet with her tears and wiped them with her hair. You gave me no kiss, but from the time I came in she has not ceased to kiss my feet. You did not anoint my head with oil, but she has anointed my feet with ointment. Therefore I tell you, her sins, which are many, are forgiven—for she loved much. But he who is forgiven little, loves little." And he said to her, "Your sins are forgiven." Then those who were at table with him began to say among themselves, "Who is this, who even forgives sins?" And he said to the woman, "Your faith has saved you; go in peace."

This woman poured out her heart to Jesus. His life, poured out for her, was a great treasure, so she loved Him in return. We also can pour out our hearts to Him in love, cherishing the value of what we've been forgiven for.

What is the value of our relationship with our God? When someone wants to know how valuable a piece of jewelry is, they take it to get appraised. The appraiser will look at it from every angle, magnifying it to see its details. Then he gives it a monetary value, showing what it would cost to buy or sell the item.

When was the last time you looked at your relationship with the Lord that way? Have you considered it from different angles, or the many details of His love and acceptance? Look at what the Lord did for you. How many ways did He suffer? How many times was He rejected? Look at the many words of love for you that are recorded in His Word. Think of what you've been forgiven for. What are the ways He has shown you His acceptance? What are the rewards He gives for those who love Him? Think of all the blessings you have received.

You are now in His family. What an inheritance!

What did it cost the Father to have you as His child? The cost was the life of His Son, Jesus Christ. The cost, like in the example of the jewelry, demonstrates its value. How valuable are you to God, then? You are as valuable as the life of His Son Jesus. Meditate on that for a while. What a truth—what a treasure!

A treasure is something that you love and that is extremely valuable to you.[8] It is of great worth to you, even if its monetary value is low. You will keep it safe and close, and look after it carefully, because it's important to your heart.

This is who God is to those who love Him—a great treasure. He is the One they keep close in their hearts. Their relationship with God is of great value to them, and they spend time looking after it, developing it, and holding it dear to them. He is the One they love, so He gets their focus. They are devoted to Him, so they remain faithful in their hearts.

For where your treasure is, there your heart will be also (Matthew 6:21 NKJV).

Do you want to love God like that, obeying the first and great commandment that Jesus spoke of? You can and you will, if you open your heart to Him—all of it. He is all-knowing, so He already knows what is in your heart. He loves and accepts you, no matter what. He is the most loving being anyone will ever know, and He wants to reveal Himself to you. Then you can love Him in return.

Hold nothing back from Him. Tear those walls down. Pour out your heart to Him. Love Him with all that you have in your heart, right now.

Yes, you can tell Him, "God, show me how much You love me. Then help me to give my whole heart to You. Teach me how to steward it well. I know it will be the safest in Your care, for You are my greatest treasure. I love You with all of my heart."

CHAPTER 3

Love God with
ALL YOUR SOUL

God needs your soul. The soul is the part that makes you "you." It is made up of your entire being: your personality, your sense of humor, your giftings, your uniqueness, your sensitivities, your quirks, your purpose, your will, your way of being you.

In religion and philosophy, the soul is the immaterial aspect or essence of a human being; that which confers individuality and humanity, often considered synonymous with the self.[9]

In Genesis 2:7 (KJV) the Bible says, *And the Lord God formed man of the dust of the ground, and breathed into his nostrils the breath of life; and man became a living soul.*

The New Life Version of the Bible says that Adam became a living "being" after God breathed into his nostrils. An important aspect of any human being's life here on earth is to become who he or she was created to be or called to be. Each person has a desire to have his or her life mean something, to make a difference. We are all looking for purpose for our lives. To find the answer to that takes self-awareness. That is part of the soul-searching of the human race: Who am I, and why am I here?

I remember a time when I read Psalm 138:8a (ESV), *The Lord will fulfill His purpose for me; your steadfast love, O Lord, endures forever.* This filled me with hope, since He was the one who would bring me into my purpose on earth. It took all the pressure off of me to figure it out, to perform, and to bring it to pass myself. Yes, I understand that I am a laborer together with God according to 1 Corinthians 3:9, so I have to do my part. However, He promised to fulfill it, so that means He will be the one responsible for bringing it to pass. Halleluiah! I do my part, and He will do the rest. I just follow His lead.

Many are the plans in a person's heart, but it is the Lord's purpose that prevails (Proverbs 19:21 NIV).

He knew me before I was born and chose me to be part of His family. He made me the way I am, to be equipped to carry out His plans for my life. When I was a classroom teacher, if I gave the students an assignment, I would give them everything they needed to complete the work as best they could. Well, our God is even better than that. Not only does He give you what you need, but He's right there with you to help you bring it to pass.

"For I know the plans I have for you," declares the Lord, "plans to prosper you and not to harm you, plans to give you hope and a future. Then you will call on me and come and pray to me, and I will listen to you" (Jeremiah 29:11-12 NIV).

And my God shall supply all your need according to His riches in glory by Christ Jesus (Philippians 4:19 NKJV).

Jesus promised that after He left, the Father would send a Helper.

But the Helper, the Holy Spirit, whom the Father will send in my name, he will teach you all things and bring to your remembrance all that I have said to you (John 14:26 ESV).

The Holy Spirit is sent to empower us for the purposes of God in our lives. As you become all that God created you to be, those around you will notice and be affected. Then you can tell them the reason why you walk in purpose and hope: our wonderful Lord and Savior.

But you shall receive power when the Holy Spirit has come upon you; and you shall be witnesses to Me in Jerusalem, and in all Judea and Samaria, and to the end of the earth (Acts 1:8 NKJV).

But sanctify the Lord God in your hearts: and be ready always to give an answer to every man that asketh you a reason of the hope that is in you with meekness and fear (1 Peter 3:15 KJV).

Pray and ask Holy Spirit to help you become all of who God created you to be. Then you can walk into your purpose and love God with all your soul.

God, who saved us and called us to a holy calling, not because of our works but because of his own purpose and grace, which he gave us in Christ Jesus before the ages began (2 Timothy 1:9 ESV).

Identity

A big part of loving God with all your soul is knowing who you are, so you can be all of who you are. Most people refer to this as your identity. Identity is the state of having unique identifying characteristics held by no other person or thing.[10]

Whenever I think of identity, Psalm 139 comes to mind.

For You formed my inward parts; you covered me in my mother's womb. I will praise You, for I am fearfully and wonderfully made; marvelous are Your works, and that my soul knows very well (Psalm 139:13-14 NKJV).

I am fearfully and wonderfully made! You are fearfully and wonderfully made! God doesn't make any mistakes, so you are wonderful, and I hope you know that very well. I pray that deep down inside, you come to like yourself. No, we are not perfect. Yes, there are some things I would like to change about myself, but that doesn't negate the good things about me, and it's the same for you.

The way you are has something to do with the way God created you. One exercise that I taught in our home group was to look at a part of you that you don't like, that annoys you or others, and that you'd like to change. Write it down. Now pray, and ask God to show you what the original quality or gift was that has been skewed from living in this world, or even stolen. Whatever comes to mind, even that fleeting thought, write it down. Whether you believe it or not, or can see any connection at all, consider what you wrote. Was there a quality that, because of something that affected you or your family, has been hidden, squelched, or even changed? Was it made fun of, thought to be a weakness, not understood, or another possibility of reactions and responses? Did you unknowingly or knowingly bury a part of you that God intended for you to walk in and to share with others?

When I was growing up, I knew a woman who was a faithful prayer warrior. I had so much respect for her, because she would pray every day for others, for hours. However, she was also very negative about people, talking to her family and friends about their problems. God showed her that He had given her discernment to see the things in people that He wanted her to pray about for them. She then realized that she had been complaining about what she saw in people to others before taking it to the Lord in prayer. She repented and changed by talking to God only, and then interceding on their behalf.

Ask God if there is something He has given you that is not being utilized at its best in your life. Let Him reveal it, then ask for forgiveness if needed, and use it for good from now on. He never takes your gifts and calling away from you. They are always there, for you to change the way you are walking in them or to pick them back up and use for His purposes. God is faithful.

God's gifts and calling can't be taken back (Romans 11:29 CEB).

In my early years of adolescence, I loved staying in bed on the weekends after I woke up. I would start praying and then see Jesus. I would then see "video-type" images of countries. It was fun! When my mom found out I was awake, she would come in and tell me to get up. After a while, I agreed with her that I needed to get up and start the day instead of lying around "daydreaming." Years later I was at a retreat, and the Lord revealed to me that it was Him showing me those images for prayer. I had shut them down because I didn't understand. I thought that it was just my imagination, and that I was wasting time. I asked Him to forgive me and said if He wanted me to see things again that I would receive them for prayer. The visions and images came back, and since then I have grown in the anointing of seeing how to pray for people, nations, and situations. He is good!

As each has received a gift, use it to serve one another, as good stewards of God's varied grace (1 Peter 4:10 ESV).

Therefore, brothers, be all the more diligent to confirm your calling and election, for if you practice these qualities you will never fall (2 Peter 1:10 ESV).

Comparison

In this day and time, it is easy to see what other people are doing and compare yourself. With social media, our exposure to people and lifestyles has multiplied exponentially. This has its benefits and pitfalls. It is wonderful to be able to stay in touch with people you know that don't live close by, or to follow someone you admire in a field to learn from their wisdom and example. However, our insecurities sometimes show up when we see someone doing what we want to do, but haven't yet. Instead of celebrating someone for their accomplishments, we can start mentally questioning ourselves, or putting ourselves down for not doing likewise. It can even become mentally abusive if we let it get too far.

But indeed, O man, who are you to reply against God? Will the thing formed say to him who formed it, "Why have you made me like this?" (Romans 9:20 NKJV).

God never intended for us to be alike, or to compare ourselves to each other. As a matter of fact, He actually states the opposite. Your individuality distinguishes you from others, and the qualities or giftings that make you unique give you your purpose. Being who God specifically created you to be is important to the Body of Christ. We need each other to be who we uniquely are.

For as in one body we have many members, and the members do not all have the same function, so we, though many, are one body in Christ, and individually members one of another. Having gifts that differ according to the grace given to us, let us use them (Romans 12:4-6a ESV).

If we are spending our time looking at others and wishing we were more like them, it takes away from us finding out who we are and spending time growing in the ways we are designed. Ask those you trust, family members or friends, what they think you are good at—not only activities, but qualities as well.

Without counsel plans fail, but with many advisers they succeed (Proverbs 15:22 ESV).

You might be good at athletics, crafts, or math, but you could also be good at being helpful, encouraging, or tenacious. Think about what brings you joy—when do you feel good about yourself, and what motivates you? What do you like to do, what qualities do you think are important, and what would you find fun and rewarding? How would you like to help others, what would you enjoy doing for the rest of your life, and what can you actually see yourself carrying out? Ask yourself these and many more questions, pondering what you get excited about, what you are interested in, and what you would be willing to spend a lot of your time and energy on. This will give you some insight into your uniqueness.

There are also multiple assessments you can take that give an evaluation according to the answers you give. These can give helpful feedback for you to look at and ponder as well. They can assist you in a journey of self-awareness and of understanding your uniqueness. The Enneagram, Myers-Briggs Personality Test, DISC Profile, and Spiritual Gifts Test are a few that you can take. The results can be very inspiring and can even encourage you to focus on an area or quality for further growth. If you've never done one before, I highly recommend it. Just know that it is not 100% truth, so don't get "hung up" on the results. Just use it as a possible tool for further individual discovery and personal growth.

Another benefit I have seen from these assessments is greater understanding of others' uniqueness as well. When I taught high school juniors, I had each student take a personal assessment or two for an assignment. The students would consistently share how they now understood why their best friend or sibling acted the way they did. Instead of their former behavior of judging or being upset with them, the students began to give grace for the ways their companions were different than them. One of my favorite days all year was when each student stood in front of the class and told their results from the personality profile, and something they had learned from it. Some students would end by apologizing for the way they had been hard on someone they didn't understand before. Others would laugh about thinking that everyone thought exactly like them, and still others were so thankful for realizing that they were not below others just because they were different than them. What a beautiful realization of the Body of Christ and the different yet equally awesome parts, all living together in unity.

When I took my children to the Indianapolis Zoo, we would enjoy the variety of animals that live there, especially because the animals are housed in a smaller model of their natural habitats. We would walk around in awe at the design of each animal and how they are so perfectly created for their environment and their need to survive. The quiet, long-legged, long-necked giraffe, for example, is tall so it can reach the tops of trees to get its food, which is plentiful because not many other animals can reach it. This is extremely different than the speedy cheetah, chasing another animal down at over sixty miles per hour to grab its food. Then there's the camel. To protect itself from the blowing sand of the desert, his nostrils can be closed to prevent the moving sand from getting in.[11] There are so many more examples of this kind of uniqueness in the animals. God gave each of them what they needed. He has amazing creativity, all for a purpose, in every creature. Why do we then think that He would not be nearly as creative in the design of the human race; that each human being should be more alike? Why don't we applaud our differences, and simply enjoy and encourage those qualities in each other that show the greatness of our Creator God? He designed you. Be all that He has made you to be. Learn to enjoy yourself and others. Discover who you are and have the liberty to be *you!*

Seeking Him

As you continue to grow in understanding who you are, love your God. How? It will look different for each of us, but one way to love God with our souls is to go after Him, to seek Him.

As for me, I would seek God, and to God would I commit my cause (Job 5:8 ESV).

How often? Always.

Seek the Lord and his strength, seek his face continually (1 Chronicles 16:11 KJV).

Even when you have not been seeking God for a while, like the Israelites in 2 Chronicles, you can always begin again to commit to loving Him, and He will come and give you rest.

For a long time Israel has been without the true God... but when in their trouble they turned to the Lord God of Israel, and sought Him, He was found by them... And all Judah rejoiced at the oath, for they had sworn with all their heart and sought Him with all their soul; and He was found by them, and the Lord gave them rest all around (2 Chronicles 15:3-4, 15 NKJV).

Seeking is a conscious effort to look for and search. When the Bible speaks of seeking God, it refers to not being satisfied with the relationship you have with Him, and so making a deliberate decision and taking action to get closer to Him.

In the path of your judgments, O Lord, we wait for you; your name and remembrance are the desire of our soul. My soul yearns for you in the night; my spirit within me earnestly seeks you (Isaiah 26:8-9 ESV).

When you are hungry or thirsty, you go get food and drink, whether you buy it, grow it, or prepare it. It is your need and desire that causes you to put in the effort. Then you eat or drink until you are satisfied. Unfortunately, it doesn't last long. On a day when I am at the computer writing, I have to take breaks to get something to eat or drink. Though I try to ignore it as long as possible, eventually I get up to fill the need so I can get back to writing without distraction.

Like with food, we are not permanently satisfied with one filling of God. He is a desire we must continually go after. As we get to know Him, He satisfies our soul. Then as we continue to live, we need and want more of Him. Our souls cry out, desiring Him to come closer and be more real to us. This craving is the need of every human soul, but it is up to each person to go after Him to fill it.

As a deer pants for flowing streams, so pants my soul for you, O God. My soul thirsts for God, for the living God. When shall I come and appear before God? (Psalm 42:1-2 ESV).

On my bed by night I sought him whom my soul loves; I sought him, but found him not. I will rise now and go about the city, in the streets and in the squares; I will seek him whom my soul loves. I sought him, but found him not. The watchmen found me as they went about in the city. "Have you seen him whom my soul loves?" Scarcely had I passed them when I found him whom my soul loves. I held him, and would not let him go (Song of Solomon 3:1-4 ESV).

In today's world, we all have times when we are seeking after things that are not God Himself. Some seek wealth, some seek acceptance, while some seek comfort and other secondary things. Having any of these things is not necessarily the problem, but where you put them in importance in your heart and soul is. They can become idols that take us away from our Lord by not putting Him first. We must lift God up above all, for He is worthy and of the highest value. All others are far less compared to Him and will fade away. We need to repent for anything that has taken that first place in our souls.

He who has clean hands and a pure heart, who does not lift up his soul to what is false and does not swear deceitfully, he will receive blessing from the Lord and righteousness from the God of his salvation. Such is the generation of those who seek him, who seek the face of the God of Jacob (Psalm 24:4-6 ESV).

Being humble is essential to seeking God. When we think we are the most important priority—number one—it can get in the way of seeking Him. It may cause us to put our efforts into building ourselves up and flaunting our achievements or possessions.

My husband actually made up a musical chorus about this. Whenever this quality was seen in someone in our home, you could guarantee that a rendition of the song would be started, and then everyone would join in. It went like this:

"I'm the center of the universe. Everything revolves around me.

I'm the center of the universe. I'm the only thing I see."

Yes, conceitedness or pride was not a quality we encouraged in our home. Pride is definitely not a quality God rewards. It deceives us into moving away from God, instead of being humble to seek Him and draw closer to Him.

For the wicked boasts of the desires of his soul, and the one greedy for gain curses and renounces the Lord (Psalm 10:3 ESV).

When pride comes, then comes disgrace, but with the humble is wisdom (Proverbs 11:2 ESV).

Humility, on the other hand, lifts God high, knowing He is to be honored and sought after.

My soul makes its boast in the Lord; let the humble hear and be glad (Psalm 34:2 ESV).

When you humble yourself before God, He will honor you.

Humble yourselves, therefore, under the mighty hand of God so that at the proper time he may exalt you (1 Peter 5:6 ESV).

For everyone who exalts himself will be humbled, and he who humbles himself will be exalted (Luke 18:14b NKJV).

When you seek the Lord, two things happen. One, He comes to you.

If you seek him, he will be found by you (2 Chronicles 15:2b ESV).

Secondly, He rewards you.

"The Lord is my portion," says my soul, "therefore I hope in Him!" The Lord is good to those who wait for Him, to the soul who seeks Him. It is good that one should hope and wait quietly for the salvation of the Lord (Lamentations 3:24-26 NKJV).

But without faith it is impossible to please Him, for he who comes to God must believe that He is, and that He is a rewarder of those who diligently seek Him (Hebrews 11:6 NKJV).

Could it be that they are the same; that the reward of seeking God is finding God Himself? You will find that in Him is everything you need and everything you want. Let your soul desire God desperately, and put effort into going after Him in your prayers and praise. Find Him in your searching in His Word. Go after Him in your thoughts and with your words. Direct your soul to follow His leading. Hold on to Him.

O God, you are my God; earnestly I seek you; my soul thirsts for you; my flesh faints for you, as in a dry and weary land where there is no water. So I have looked upon you in the sanctuary, beholding your power and glory. Because your steadfast love is better than life, my lips will praise you. So I will bless you as long as I live; in your name I will lift up my hands. My soul will be satisfied as with fat and rich food, and my mouth will praise you with joyful lips, when I remember you upon my bed, and meditate on you in the watches of the night; for you have been my help, and in the shadow of your wings I will sing for joy. My soul clings to you; your right hand upholds me (Psalm 63:1-8 ESV).

Whenever you find yourself seeking after other things, return to God. He is always there to love you and lift you up.

But from there you will seek the Lord your God and you will find him, if you search after him with all your heart and with all your soul. When you are in tribulation, and all these things come upon you in the latter days, you will return to the Lord your God and obey his voice (Deuteronomy 4:29-30 ESV).

Praise and Worship

As you seek Him and see His great worth, your love will overflow through praise and worship. It is a joyful benefit of your love for Him.

When Mary, the mother of Jesus, went to visit her cousin Elizabeth, their conversation led to Mary praising God from her soul.

And Mary said, "My soul magnifies the Lord" (Luke 1:46 ESV).

David, in the book of Psalms, writes: *Bless the Lord, O my soul, and all that is within me, bless His holy name!* (Psalm 103:1 ESV).

David was a man after God's heart, and he praised God with everything that he was. He used his words, songs, instruments, and dance—all expressions from within—to give God glory and love. Here are a few of his words praising the Lord from his soul.

To you, O Lord, I lift up my soul (Psalm 25:1 NKJV).

My soul will rejoice in the Lord, exulting in his salvation (Psalm 35:9 ESV).

I will bless the Lord at all times; His praise shall continually be in my mouth. My soul shall make its boast in the Lord; the humble shall hear of it and be glad. Oh, magnify the Lord with me, and let us exalt His name together (Psalm 34:1-3 NKJV).

During worship at a church service, I looked around to see a woman dancing before Him. I noticed another sitting quietly in her seat, head bowed and eyes closed. Then there was a gentleman behind me praying with someone who was crying, another reading his Bible, and another standing, singing loudly with the music. I could continue about the different actions and responses I saw going on in the room during this awe-filled time of worship to our God, but none of them were out of order or showy. To me, it showed the differences and preferences in God's wonderful people to worship Him and show Him their unique love. It was beautiful! So, ask Him to help you be who He created you to be, and then give it back to Him in your wonderful way of praising and worshiping Him. Go be with the One you love.

One thing I have desired of the Lord, that will I seek: that I may dwell in the house of the Lord all the days of my life, to behold the beauty of the Lord, and to inquire in His temple (Psalm 27:4 NKJV).

Troubled Soul

There are times when our souls are troubled from the circumstances of life. The weight our souls may carry from unrest, sickness, and the pressures that surround us can be very heavy. Sometimes we don't even know what the cause is, yet other times the problem is obvious. It can be personal, or we may be troubled by the problem of a friend, or it may even be conflict that is going on in the world around us. Whatever the reason, our souls sense the pressure, the injustice, the sorrow, and the pain. Some things cannot just be fixed, and we may not know what to do about it. It can be frustrating and even depressing. Our souls can be pressed down, anxious, and in great turmoil.

I loathe my life; I will give free utterance to my complaint; I will speak in the bitterness of my soul (Job 10:1 ESV).

In Psalm 6 (ESV), we see David crying out to the Lord in distress over persecution from his enemies. He was weary, he was grieved, and he was weak. Read the detail of his honesty when pouring out his troubles in this Psalm, but also notice how many times he uses the name of the Lord while doing it.

1 *O Lord, rebuke me not in your anger, nor discipline me in your wrath.*

2 *Be gracious to me, O Lord, for I am languishing; heal me, O Lord, for my bones are troubled.*

3 *My soul also is greatly troubled. But you, O Lord—how long?*

4 *Turn, O Lord, deliver my life; save me for the sake of your steadfast love.*

5 *For in death there is no remembrance of you; in Sheol who will give you praise?*

6 *I am weary with my moaning; every night I flood my bed with tears; I drench my couch with my weeping.*

7 *My eye wastes away because of grief; it grows weak because of all my foes.*

8 *Depart from me, all you workers of evil, for the Lord has heard the sound of my weeping.*

9 *The Lord has heard my plea; the Lord accepts my prayer.*

10 *All my enemies shall be ashamed and greatly troubled; they shall turn back and be put to shame in a moment.*

As troubled as David was, we see that he knew where to go for help. He didn't run to people; he honestly cried out to his God. He went again and again, holding nothing back. He was real, and we can be too.

Jesus was the same way. He went to the Father in troubled times.

And they went to a place called Gethsemane. And he said to his disciples, "Sit here while I pray." And he took with him Peter and James and John, and began to be greatly distressed and troubled. And he said to them, "My soul is very sorrowful, even to death. Remain here and watch." And going a little farther, he fell on the ground and prayed that, if it were possible, the hour might pass from him. And he said, "Abba, Father, all things are possible for you. Remove this cup from me. Yet not what I will, but what you will" (Mark 14:32-36 ESV).

The pressure of knowing that He would carry the sins of the world and would be tortured and crucified had to be extremely intense. It was so intense that Jesus sweat drops of blood during this prayer in the Garden.

And being in agony he prayed more earnestly; and his sweat became like great drops of blood falling down to the ground (Luke 22:44 ESV).

According to Dr. Frederick Zugibe, Chief Medical Examiner of Rockland County, New York, the clinical term for what happened to Jesus in this verse is *hematohidrosis.*

"Around the sweat glands, there are multiple blood vessels in a net-like form. Under the pressure of great stress, the vessels constrict. Then as the anxiety passes the blood vessels dilate to the point of rupture. The blood goes into the sweat glands. As the sweat glands are producing a lot of sweat, it pushes the blood to the surface—coming out as droplets of blood mixed with sweat."[12]

Jesus was under great stress, but He poured it out to His Father, who sent an angel to strengthen him.

And there appeared to him an angel from heaven, strengthening him (Luke 22:43 ESV).

God can and will strengthen us as well, as we come to Him with our troubles.

Come to me, all who labor and are heavy laden, and I will give you rest. Take my yoke upon you, and learn from me, for I am gentle and lowly in heart, and you will find rest for your souls. For my yoke is easy, and my burden is light (Matthew 11:28-30 ESV).

Come to Him, just as you are, like Jesus did. Come to Him and pray. Don't hold back. Pour it all out, and let

God lift you up. He is faithful, and He has promised to restore you.

My soul melts from heaviness; strengthen me according to Your word (Psalm 119:28 NKJV).

The Lord is my shepherd; I shall not want. He makes me lie down in green pastures. He leads me beside still waters. He restores my soul (Psalm 23:1-3a ESV).

Hope

There is a characteristic of the soul that exemplifies to me both strength and courage in this troubled world, and that is *hope*. The dictionary defines the verb *hope* this way: "to desire with expectation of obtainment or fulfillment."[13] Hope implies waiting for something to happen in the future; yet not just waiting, but waiting with a longing, trusting that it will happen. When you do not see the outcome yet, but believe for a desired result even when the circumstances may be saying something different, that is absolutely courageous and takes strength.

Be strong and let your heart take courage, all you who hope in the LORD (Psalm 31:24 NASB).

Having hope affects how we see things, how we speak, and how we act. When others may be giving up, accepting their circumstances, and saying what is, those that hope are seeing above the circumstances, and holding on to a better outcome, and saying so. This takes faith as well.

Now faith is the substance of things hoped for, the evidence of things not seen (Hebrews 11:1 NKJV).

Our son was six weeks premature when he was born. At the hospital, the doctor sat down with us and told us some things that did not seem right. He then listed all the things that could be wrong with our son and the long-term health problems that he could have. My husband and I decided that we could either believe what the doctor said, or we could believe that our son was going to be healthy and whole. We held on to the hope that God would make our son whole. It almost became fun each time the doctor came back and said, "You can check that one off the list. There's no problem with that." Our son was discharged from the hospital healthy, except for a minor breathing issue that he soon outgrew. According to the nurses, he was sent home in record time. That was a fulfillment of our hope in God to have a healthy son.

True hope is a characteristic of the Christian faith, where our expectation is not in an outcome or thing, but in a being—God, who brings the outcome to pass. He is the source of true hope.

Now the God of hope fill you with all joy and peace in believing, that ye may abound in hope, through the power of the Holy Ghost (Romans 15:13 KJV).

When life gets tough and your soul gets weary, do what it takes to put your hope in God, who will fill you with joy, peace, faith, and wholeness.

Why are you cast down, O my soul, and why are you in turmoil within me? Hope in God; for I shall again praise him, my salvation and my God.

This verse is recorded three times in Psalms: Psalm 42:5, 42:11, and 43:5 (ESV). The psalmist told his soul more than once to not be down, but to put hope in God as His salvation, and to praise Him.

The Word of God provides hope, so look to the Scriptures in times of need.

You are my shelter and my shield; I put my hope in your word (Psalm 119:114 CSB).

I believe that the Lord inspired me to list below some of the Psalms that speak about hope and God. The Word of God provides hope to the soul. I pray that as you read these, hope will fill your soul and give you strength for a brighter future.

No one who hopes in you will ever be put to shame (Psalm 25:3a NIV).

Guide me in your truth and teach me, for you are God my Savior, and my hope is in you all day long (Psalm 25:5 NIV).

May integrity and uprightness protect me, because my hope, Lord, is in you (Psalm 25:21 NIV).

We wait in hope for the Lord; he is our help and our shield (Psalm 33:20 NIV).

May your unfailing love be with us, Lord, even as we put our hope in you (Psalm 33:22 NIV).

Rest in God alone, my soul, for my hope comes from him (Psalm 62:5 CSB).

Happy is the one whose help is the God of Jacob, whose hope is in the Lord his God, the Maker of heaven and earth, the sea and everything in them. He remains faithful forever (Psalm 146:5-6 CSB).

The Lord reminded me of this analogy. My family and I were vacationing on a lake in Michigan one summer, and we had thrown the anchor over the side of the boat in the middle of the lake. Though the waves kept pounding against the boat and we were being rocked aggressively inside, the anchor held on. Ever since then I think of hope as "Holding On to the Promised Expectation" (H.O.P.E.), no matter what circumstances are pounding my life. I can be like a pit bull I knew who would bite down on something and not let it go. If there is a situation that needs prayer, I ask the Lord for a verse to hold on to and keep praying it for His outcome. I am holding on to Him while speaking the truth of His Word in prayer. No matter how rocky the situation, I do not let go of the promise He gave me. You can too!

When God desired to show more convincingly to the heirs of the promise the unchangeable character of his purpose, he guaranteed it with an oath, so that by two unchangeable things, in which it is impossible for God to lie, we who have fled for refuge might have strong encouragement to hold fast to the hope set before us. We have this as a sure and steadfast anchor of the soul, a hope that enters into the inner place be-

hind the curtain, where Jesus has gone as a forerunner on our behalf (Hebrews 6:17-20a ESV).

God is faithful and does what He says, so when I need help I can anchor my soul to hope for better things to come, no matter the circumstances. Jesus went before us to the heavens and is now making intercession for us, so my hope and faith are even stronger now that I am partnered with my Savior and Lord.

Christ Jesus is the one who died, but even more, has been raised; he also is at the right hand of God and intercedes for us (Romans 8:34b CSB).

Blessed is the man who trusts in the Lord, and whose hope is the Lord (Jeremiah 17:7 NKJV).

Our soul waits for the Lord; he is our help and our shield (Psalm 33:20 ESV).

How can you love God with all your soul? You can ask Him to help you be who He created you to be. He understands you—all of you—your personality and strengths, your hopes and dreams, and even your shortcomings. Yet He created you with a purpose and a calling for good works.

For we are his workmanship, created in Christ Jesus for good works, which God prepared beforehand, that we should walk in them (Ephesians 2:10 ESV).

He will help you to discover and walk in them as you seek Him. Then you can commit your ways to Him in worship, in seeking Him, and in living for Him with hope, no matter what you're experiencing. Love Him with all your soul.

Beloved, I pray that you may prosper in all things and be healthy, even as your soul prospers (3 John 2 WEB).

CHAPTER 4

Love God with
ALL YOUR MIND

God desires your mind. The mind is referred to as the faculty of consciousness and thought,[14] so it is the center of understanding, reasoning, decision-making, and imagination. We can certainly understand how this is an important part of living the First and Great Commandment. To reason that loving God needs to be our first priority, and then deciding to take some actions to grow in our love for Him, would be an important use of our mind. We're all at different stages, but can you imagine how you would do this?

A trail of thinking can begin by an observation, a conversation, information from something read or heard, something experienced or felt, or even just from a random thought from within a person. He or she may ponder the data, reflect on it for a while, and then either make a decision or just stop thinking about it. This may even lead to a corresponding action. How long a person continues to think about a topic is really up to them. A person's focus of thought can change to another topic any time, either by their own decision or by random causes.

When I was younger, my mind would go anywhere it wanted. I did not try to direct it or in any way control it. You can imagine the disaster that was. My thoughts were determined by the circumstances, my feelings, other people, and the information I was taking in. Sometimes they were up, sometimes they were down, and sometimes they were swirling all around. I was definitely on a roller coaster, with confusion as the driver.

Then I took a Bible class that showed me a better way to live. The truth in Romans 12:2 (NKJV) was eye-opening to me.

And do not be conformed to this world, but be transformed by the renewing of your mind, that you may prove what is that good and acceptable and perfect will of God.

The teacher taught that the word transformed was like the metamorphosis a caterpillar goes through to become a butterfly. I was amazed! I thought, *I could change that drastically by the changing of my mind? I can stop crawling around in the dirt of life and fly above it?* I definitely wanted and needed that kind of freedom. To also read in that verse that this would show me what God's will was for my life was an added incentive to get started.

I began reading the Bible, studying it, taking classes, and listening to people expounding the Scriptures. I had heard the stories of biblical heroes and Jesus' life many times, but I didn't know there were so many power-packed verses on how to live this life that Christ came and died for us to have. Being a Christian before this was good, but transforming to actually "be" what the Bible says I can be was amazing! The peace that flooded my mind because I was thinking what the Word said about me dramatically changed me. It can do the same for you. The differences between a caterpillar and a butterfly are huge, and that is what can happen for all of us when we put the thoughts of God in our minds. We do not need to crawl around on the ground—slowly trying to not get stepped on—anymore. We can fly freely with beautiful, colored wings, as the Spirit of God takes us to new heights. Then our minds will have the freedom to love God fully.

Negativity

For as [a man] thinks... so is he (Proverbs 23:7 NKJV).

Remember that the mind is an area of each person that Jesus said to love God with, but if my mind is being used to keep up with what's going on in the world, what I have to do, and what I can learn on social media, is there any room for thoughts of God in a day? Your own thinking can be somewhat directed or controlled. Yet this is a skill that is learned through teaching or circumstances. When babies are born, their needs usually trigger their responses, like crying when hungry or tired. As children grow, the parents can train them to communicate in different ways. Like when my grandson was getting older, his parents trained him to go to bed at a certain time, not crying when trying to fall asleep. There are at times medical reasons—whether physical, emotional, or mental—why some people have a harder time controlling their thinking and may need some kind of intervention. However, the majority of people can learn how to focus their minds on what they need or choose to. This is a process that can be easier at some times than others. For example, if I am tired or experiencing a stressful time in my life, it is harder to focus and think positively about a situation. Our minds can be affected by a variety of influences, both internal and external. That's why it is important to make wise choices in areas where you can influence your thinking. For example, exercise and healthy eating can assist you with good thinking, because they help you feel good.

On the contrary, taking unnecessary drugs or being involved in a harmful relationship can definitely affect a person negatively, causing thought patterns that can pull a person down. Of course, there are at times negative influences that you may have no control over, but hopefully they are temporary, and you can either get the help you need or wait and pray for them to change.

There was a time in my life when the circumstances that were causing me stress were hard to get away from, so after talking with family, I decided to move. This was one way to alleviate the pressures around me and get a new start, with my mind free from negativity. It worked. A new environment was just what I needed to uplift my thought life to focus on hope and peace. This and other decisions are the kinds we all need to make at different times in our lives to help our minds be free of pressure, fear, anxiety, depression, or any number of other negative thought patterns. We can't always do this on our own. We may need to talk to someone who will help us to choose options that keep our minds healthy, whole and happy. This is an important part of helping us to be our best, so we can love God with all of our mind.

I used to say that the two great commandments Jesus spoke of in Matthew, Mark, and Luke were to love God and love your neighbor. That is, until the day when I felt the Holy Spirit nudge me to go to my Bible to look it up. There I read, *You shall love the Lord your God with all your heart, with all your soul, with all your mind, and with all your strength, and your neighbor as yourself.* As yourself? Wait a minute. This says I am to love my neighbor as I love myself. Wow, part of the commandment is to love myself? I never thought of that as a commandment God wanted me to obey. At that time in my life, it was easier for me to love others than it was to love myself, but that is what Jesus said to do, so I had to start.

We demolish arguments and every pretension that sets itself up against the knowledge of God, and we take captive every thought to make it obedient to Christ (2 Corinthians 10:5 NIV).

I got a journal and began writing down my negative thoughts about myself. Then I would cross them out and write an opposite, positive thought from the Word of God to replace it, like *"I can do all things through Christ who strengthens me,"* and *"I am fearfully and wonderfully made."* I started reading those aloud in front of a mirror. At first it was very difficult and awkward. I could barely even look at myself, but as I kept doing it, I eventually started believing what I was saying. I finally got to the place where I could even smile while looking at myself and say those truths with boldness and confidence. I was being transformed by the renewing of my mind.

The Bible even tells us that since we've accepted Christ, our old life is dead, and we have a new life in God. Therefore, we can decide to not focus on earthly things, but to set our thoughts on things above.

If then you were raised with Christ, seek those things which are above, where Christ is, sitting at the right hand of God. Set your mind on things above, not on things on the earth. For you died, and your life is hidden with Christ in God (Colossians 3:1-3 NKJV).

If we stopped thinking about earthly, negative things, that could give us a lot more time to focus on God. I remember when I was first dating my husband. We were at college, and I was in the library trying to study, but my mind kept thinking about him and wondering what he was doing. I was definitely not getting much work done, so I went and found him in his dorm. We just sat together, talking and enjoying each other for a while. Then, when I went back to the library, I could focus on what I was doing. Could it be that if we talked more with the One we love, we could have a more fruitful life? Loving God with our minds will reap great benefits.

Fear or Faith

Another area of thinking that produced abundant fruit for me was getting rid of fear. Honestly, I did not even realize how much fear I was living in and how much it was affecting my decisions and actions. I was afraid of making decisions because I didn't want to be wrong. I was afraid of speaking up if I disagreed, because I didn't want people to get mad or upset at me. I was afraid of change, because I didn't know where it would take me. It seemed safe to just keep things the way they were and to keep doing things the same way all the time. I realized that I was trying to secure my own safety to avoid the fear of the unknown. However, there is very little growth when there is no change. Practically, God was not my fortress; I was—and not a good one, either.

When I am afraid, I put my trust in you. In God, whose word I praise, in God I trust; I shall not be afraid. What can flesh do to me? (Psalm 56:3-4 ESV).

In peace I will both lie down and sleep; for you alone, O Lord, make me dwell in safety (Psalm 4:8 ESV).

Fear was something that I saw in my family at times, but I didn't realize it could be passed down from previous generations until I heard someone teach on it. It can also be passed on to the following generations, and that was something I did not want to do. Therefore, I went to a prayer and ministry seminar to learn how to break fear off my family line.

And now, please let the power of the Lord be great as you have promised, saying, "The Lord is slow to anger and abounding in steadfast love, forgiving iniquity and transgression, but he will by no means clear the guilty, visiting the iniquity of the fathers on the children, to the third and the fourth generation." Please pardon the iniquity of this people, according to the greatness of your steadfast love, just as you have forgiven this people, from Egypt until now. Then the Lord said, "I have pardoned, according to your word" (Numbers 14:17-20 ESV).

I was taught to not only confess my own sins, but also those of my ancestors. Not knowing their specific sins didn't matter; I repented for their fear as well as mine, and forgave them for passing it on to me.

The Israelites separated themselves from all foreigners and stood and confessed their sins and the iniquities of their fathers (Nehemiah 9:2 ESV).

If we say we have no sin, we deceive ourselves, and the truth is not in us. If we confess our sins, he is faithful and just to forgive us our sins and to cleanse us from all unrighteousness (1 John 1:8-9 ESV).

After the prayer time I heard the Holy Spirit say, "You just broke off fear that has been in your generational line for a hundred years." I was surprised, but honestly, I could feel the difference. Something had changed in me, and there was a new sense of relief. Truly, God had set me free!

And ye shall know the truth, and the truth shall make you free (John 8:32 KJV).

I had once heard that fear was "**F**alse **E**vidence **A**ppearing **R**eal" (FEAR). That rang so true to me now. I realized that I had been believing what the circumstances looked like, instead of holding on to God's truths and trusting Him to change my circumstances. If truth is actually true, then logically, anything that contradicts it is false. The Word of God is truth (John 17:17), so therefore it is true. If my circumstance looks different than the Word of God, then it is false evidence appearing real. This is what was causing fear in my life—false evidence. I decided to think and speak the truth from the Bible over my negative circumstances and then watch what God would do. Even when I didn't see the change, it changed my perspective, which got rid of fear. Speaking and holding on to truth would actually be faith. Hebrews 11:1 (NKJV) states:

Now faith is the substance of things hoped for, the evidence of things not seen.

Jesus demonstrated and taught us how to live this way. He showed us to speak directly to a negative situation, believing it will change.

Now in the morning, as He returned to the city, He was hungry. And seeing a fig tree by the road, He came to it and found nothing on it but leaves, and said to it, "Let no fruit grow on you ever again." Immediately the fig tree withered away. And when the disciples saw it, they marveled, saying, "How did the fig tree wither away so soon?" So Jesus answered and said to them, "Assuredly, I say to you, if you have faith and do not doubt, you will not only do what was done to the fig tree, but also if you say to this mountain, 'Be removed and be cast into the sea,' it will be done. And whatever things you ask in prayer, believing, you will receive" (Matthew 21: 18-22 NKJV).

He also prayed for us in John 17.

Verses 15-17 (NKJV), *I do not pray that You should take them out of the world, but that You should keep them from the evil one. They are not of the world, just as I am not of the world. Sanctify them by Your truth. Your word is truth.*

God's truths are greater than all our circumstances. His faith will grow in us, and His love will overcome all our fears.

So faith comes from hearing, and hearing through the word of Christ (Romans 10:17 ESV).

Love has been perfected among us in this: that we may have boldness in the day of judgment; because as He is, so are we in this world. There is no fear in love; but perfect love casts out fear, because fear involves torment. But he who fears has not been made perfect in love. We love Him because He first loved us (1 John 4:17-19 NKJV).

Notice the phrase from this verse: "as He is, so are we in this world." The verb "is" is in the present tense, so it means like Jesus is *right now.* How is Jesus right now? He is sitting at the right hand of the Father in His glorified body! He has defeated death and all earthly circumstances and is making intercession for us (Romans 8:34). If this verse just said we are to be like Him as He is, that would be amazing, but the verse is very clear that we are to be like Him while we are in this life. This is how we are to be *in this world,* not just when we get to heaven. Read that again. As He is, *so are we* in this world! Yes, we are in this world, but not of it. We are citizens of heaven (Philippians 3:20). The way Jesus is right now is the way we are *right now*. You are a beloved child of God, more than a conqueror through Him who loves us, accepted, chosen, forgiven, redeemed, an heir of salvation, and His ambassador.

An ambassador represents the nation or dignitary that sent him or her. This ambassador ought to enjoy all the privileges and rights which his/her master himself, as a sovereign, would have. Therefore, certain privileges are given to the ambassador which are not attributed to other persons living there. Also, ambassadors are not subject to the laws of the land to which they are sent, so that nation cannot proceed against them according to the ordinary course of justice there. Even though they live in a different land, they are legally under the jurisdiction of the land from which they came. These are some of the privileges given to an ambassador.[15]

Since we are ambassadors of Jesus Christ, we have the rights and privileges of heaven. We do not live under the jurisdiction of earth, but of heaven. That is why we look to the truths of the Bible to discover what our lives should look like. We renew our minds to the truths of the Word of God and declare those to be our standard of living. There will always be an enemy who wants to pull us under the lies of this world, but legally, we have an advocate—a defense attorney—Jesus Christ, who goes to the throne room of heaven and pleads our case to the Righteous Judge, who happens to be our heavenly Father. Then the righteousness of the kingdom of heaven is the standard that everything is compared to when a verdict is declared. The truths of God's Word about me are the rights and privileges that I live under, believe, and declare, now and forever. Speak to your fig tree, your mountain, your false evidence, and tell it to go. Then call in the outcome of heaven over your life, and hold on to the picture of that truth coming into reality for you. That is what Jesus showed us to do, and He is helping us to live it.

My little children, I am writing these things to you so that you may not sin. But if anyone does sin, we have an advocate with the Father, Jesus Christ the righteous (1 John 2:1 ESV).

God will surely take care of His own, no matter what you are walking through.

The Lord is my shepherd; I shall not want. He makes me lie down in green pastures. He leads me beside still waters. He restores my soul. He leads me in paths of righteousness for his name's sake. Even though I walk through the valley of the shadow of death, I will fear no evil, for you are with me; your rod and your staff, they comfort me. You prepare a table before me in the presence of my enemies; you anoint my head with oil; my cup overflows. Surely goodness and mercy shall follow me all the days of my life, and I shall dwell in the house of the Lord forever (Psalm 23:1-6 ESV).

The chorus of the song "I Will Fear No More" by the Afters is a great declaration to speak or sing about our choice to love and trust God and to not live in fear or worry.

> You're my courage when I worry in the dead of
>   night.
> You're my strength 'cause I'm not strong enough
>   to win this fight.
> You are greater than the battle raging in my
>   mind.
> I will trust You, Lord, I will fear no more.[16]

I sought the Lord, and he answered me and delivered me from all my fears (Psalm 34:4 ESV).

Fear is not from God, and He has empowered you to overcome it with His power, with His love, and with thoughts that line up with life and truth. Fear is not the kind of fruit you want to grow in your life, so speak God's truths to any fear, like Jesus did to the fig tree.

Then watch it wither away as you overcome it with faith, love, and power.

For God has not given us a spirit of fear, but of power and of love and of a sound mind (2 Timothy 1:7 NKJV).

For this is the love of God, that we keep his commandments. And his commandments are not burdensome. For everyone who has been born of God overcomes the world. And this is the victory that has overcome the world—our faith. Who is it that overcomes the world except the one who believes that Jesus is the Son of God? (1 John 5:3-5 ESV).

Anxiety

Anxiety or worry is another avenue of negative thinking that can distract us from our love for God. Many people experience stress and anxiety from time to time, usually based on something going on in their life. They may have a hard time not dwelling on the difficulties or problems. Others may have anxiety from chemical or hormonal imbalances. Either way, anxiety causes a sense of apprehension and can interfere with normal activities. Jesus warned us that there would be trouble, but also assured us that He is bigger than all our troubles. As we stay close to Him, we can have peace.

I have said these things to you, that in me you may have peace. In the world you will have tribulation. But take heart; I have overcome the world (John 16:33 ESV).

Uncertainty and the unknown are going to be part of life on this earth, but it doesn't necessarily mean there will automatically be problems. Though life can be uncertain, our God is certainly faithful to show up and help us in times of need.

And Jesus said to his disciples, "Therefore I tell you, do not be anxious about your life, what you will eat, nor about your body, what you will put on. For life is more than food, and the body more than clothing. Consider the ravens: they neither sow nor reap, they have neither storehouse nor barn, and yet God feeds them. Of how much more value are you than the birds! And which of you by being anxious can add a single hour to his span of life? If then you are not able to do as small a thing as that, why are you anxious about the rest? Consider the lilies, how they grow: they neither toil nor spin, yet I tell you, even Solomon in all his glory was not arrayed like one of these. But if God so clothes the grass, which is alive in the field today, and tomorrow is thrown into the oven, how much more will he clothe you, O you of little faith! And do not seek what you are to eat and what you are to drink, nor be worried. For all the nations of the world seek after these things, and your

Father knows that you need them. Instead, seek his kingdom, and these things will be added to you" (Luke 12:22-31 ESV).

Anxiety robs you of a life of peace, but He gives you something else to do when you start having worried or anxious thoughts. Go to Him! Spend time with God, love Him, praise Him, talk with Him, and ask Him questions. Pray and tell Him what you want, thanking Him. He will give you His peace, which will be like a fence, guarding your mind and heart. This peace is higher than your understanding of the situation, because His ways and thoughts are always greater and higher than ours.

Do not be anxious about anything, but in everything by prayer and supplication with thanksgiving let your requests be made known to God. And the peace of God, which surpasses all understanding, will guard your hearts and your minds in Christ Jesus (Philippians 4:6-7 ESV).

For as the heavens are higher than the earth, so are my ways higher than your ways and my thoughts than your thoughts (Isaiah 55:9 ESV).

A key is not to take back the worry after you've prayed. Jesus told us to bind or tie up things on earth we don't want, and then loose or release the good. Don't let the keys sit on the shelf. Use binding and loosing to bring the things of heaven to your life. This may take some practice, but continue to replace the negative concerns with thoughts of peace, knowing that His provision is coming in due season.

And I will give you the keys of the kingdom of heaven, and whatever you bind on earth will be bound in heaven, and whatever you loose on earth will be loosed in heaven (Matthew 16:19 NKJV).

Many times when I am overly concerned about something—yes, even worried—I put some soft worship music on and relax. Then I hand the concern over to Jesus or throw it up for Him to catch. I open my arms and ask Him to give me His good gifts instead. It is the sweetest time with Him and always relieves my anxious thoughts.

God and His answers to our situations are worth waiting for. Take your negative, anxious, fearful, frustrated, depressed thoughts to Him, and let them go like a helium balloon soaring up, up, up, until you see them no more. Then ask the Holy Spirit to fill you back up with His life-giving fruits of love, joy, peace, patience, goodness, gentleness, meekness, faith, and self-control. Let the fruit of His presence be your sweet reward for turning things over to Him.

Peace

As people we want to live our lives with peace, even though we know our lives are not perfect. In the middle of life, with all its problems, concerns, ups, and downs, we want to be able to rest, be at peace, and relax. So, what works for you? That's what you need to find out. Does putting on music—whether it's praise and worship music, dance music, or peaceful instrumental— help you to find peace? Does going for a walk or run, looking at nature, and getting away from your daily environment help you? How about reading a book, or watching a movie that makes you laugh or try to figure out the ending; do those things cause you to relax? Playing with children or an animal is often an activity that can bring joy and peace. There are a number of things you can do that will help your mind relax. Finding out what it is that causes your mind to become peaceful is important.

Then you can begin praying, talking to, or thinking about God. Ask Him whatever you want, because just talking to Him helps to calm the anxious or troubled mind.

He will keep in perfect peace all those who trust in him, whose thoughts turn often to the Lord! (Isaiah 26:3 TLB).

In the world, peace means a lack of conflict, violence, and war. It is a concept that refers to harmony and security, which are dependent on circumstances between people, people groups, or nations. However, peace is far more than a calm environment on the outside or a lack of problems. Real peace comes from God.

Peace I leave with you, My peace I give to you; not as the world gives do I give to you. Let not your heart be troubled, neither let it be afraid (John 14:27 NKJV).

By the saving work of Christ on the cross, the people of God have come into a relationship of peace with God Himself, who is the source of peace. When Christ died, He took our sins so we could be blameless and righteous. Then we could be reconciled or brought back together with God as our Father, so we will live eternally with Him in love and peace.

May God himself, the God of peace, sanctify you through and through. May your whole spirit, soul and body be kept blameless at the coming of our Lord Jesus Christ (1 Thessalonians 5:23 NIV).

This kind of peace is not of this world. It is a spiritual reality of God's kingdom, but it can be lived out here and now by knowing and focusing on Him, even in the midst of problems. It is a blessing, knowing that the Lord of heaven and earth is watching over you and will take care of you, now and forever.

For those who live according to the flesh set their minds on the things of the flesh, but those who live according to the Spirit set their minds on the things of the Spirit. For to set the mind on the flesh is death, but to set the mind on the Spirit is life and peace (Romans 8:5-6 ESV).

To those who through the righteousness of our God and Savior Jesus Christ have received a faith as precious as ours: Grace and peace be yours in abundance through the knowledge of God and of Jesus our Lord. His divine power has given us everything we need for a godly life through our knowledge of him who called us by his own glory and goodness (2 Peter 1:1-3 NIV).

God does not just give the quality of peace, but He gave us the Prince of Peace, Jesus Christ.

For to us a child is born, to us a son is given; and the government shall be upon his shoulder, and his name shall be called Wonderful Counselor, Mighty God, Everlasting Father, Prince of Peace (Isaiah 9:6 ESV).

When someone accepts Jesus as their Lord and Savior, the Prince of Peace takes residence in them. Colossians 1:27 (KJV), *Christ IN YOU, the hope of glory.* We not only have peace living in us, but we are the peacemakers as well.

Blessed are the peacemakers, for they shall be called sons of God (Matthew 5:9 NKJV).

As peacemakers, we can have an impact on people and circumstances around us. However, it depends on us. Whenever there are storms in our lives, we have been given the authority in the name of Jesus Christ to speak peace to them and change the outcome. It is His power that is able to make things happen, but we have to do our part, since we are co-laborers with Him. In relationships, we are the ones who have to take the higher ground to bless and not curse, forgive and reconcile, speak truth and honor, and show Jesus to a hurting world. Let who's on the inside of you come out.

Repay no one evil for evil, but give thought to do what is honorable in the sight of all. If possible, so far as it depends on you, live peaceably with all (Romans 12:17-18 ESV).

And he awoke and rebuked the wind and said to the sea, "Peace! Be still!" And the wind ceased, and there was a great calm (Mark 4:39 ESV).

There will always be trouble in this life as long as Satan, the enemy of God, is still allowed to roam the earth. However, we can resist him and his tactics, because greater is He that is in us. We also know from Scripture that Satan's end is coming, so don't allow your mind to be bombarded with discouragement or deception. Keep your thoughts on things above.

And every spirit that confesseth not that Jesus Christ is come in the flesh is not of God: and this is that spirit of antichrist, whereof ye have heard that it should come; and even now already is it in the world. Ye are of God, little children, and have overcome them: because greater is he that is in you, than he that is in the world (1 John 4:3-4 KJV).

Be sober, be vigilant; because your adversary the devil walks about like a roaring lion, seeking whom he may devour. Resist him, steadfast in the faith, knowing that the same sufferings are experienced by your brotherhood in the world (1 Peter 5:8-9 NKJV).

The God of peace will soon crush Satan under your feet. The grace of our Lord Jesus Christ be with you (Romans 16:20 ESV).

We have been called to a life that far exceeds what we can think or even imagine. Ephesians 3:20 is my life's verse. I love it! God can do far more than we think He can, and it's according to the power in us. Therefore, I set my thoughts on what the Word of God says, and speak out that He can do more. EAAAYAT is my acronym: Exceedingly Abundantly Above All You Ask/Think.

May be able to comprehend with all the saints what is the width and length and depth and height—to know the love of Christ which passes knowledge; that you may be filled with all the fullness of God. Now to Him who is able to do exceedingly abundantly above all that we ask or think, according to the power that works in us (Ephesians 3:18-20 NKJV).

Receive His peace and fill your thoughts with the Word. Then bring His peace to others, expecting Him to do more. EAAAYAT!

Thankful

When I love someone, I think about what I am thankful for in our relationship. I consider what I appreciate about them instead of focusing on things that I don't like. I also remember what I am grateful for from our past—times they have blessed me, things they did for me, ways they showed kindness and love. I remember the good times. This thankfulness then helps my love for them to grow and affects how I treat them. Being thankful influences loving feelings and behaviors.

Being thankful in a relationship doesn't bring perfection, though. You can be grateful for your spouse or a child and still be mad at them for something in the moment. It's harder, though, to stay upset with them when you start thinking of how thankful you are for them. Thoughts of gratitude can lessen the negativity and put it in perspective, helping you to think about the bigger picture. Being thankful can also give you a reason to pick yourself up and keep going forward when you have a setback or are disillusioned.

Harvard Health Publishing, in their article "In Praise of Gratitude," stated: "In positive psychology research, gratitude is strongly and consistently associated with greater happiness. Gratitude helps people feel more positive emotions, relish good experiences, improve their health, deal with adversity, and build strong relationships."[17]

Even in our relationship with God, thankfulness is important. It helps to keep our thoughts positive toward Him, even when we might be struggling. You may not feel thankful, but if you begin to think and speak words of thanksgiving to Him, you are obeying His Word, and your heart will eventually follow.

And above all these put on love, which binds everything together in perfect harmony. And let the peace of Christ rule in your hearts, to which indeed you were called in one body. And be thankful. Let the word of Christ dwell in you richly, teaching and admonishing one another in all wisdom, singing psalms and hymns and spiritual songs, with thankfulness in your hearts to God. And whatever you do, in word or deed, do everything in the name of the Lord Jesus, giving thanks to God the Father through him (Colossians 3:14-20 ESV).

Whether you feel like it or not, you can make a decision to call out to God and speak words of thanksgiving to Him. It may not feel genuine, but it will be a sacrifice to Him, submitting to what the Bible says to do. Then over time, it can become genuine and true for you. Be thankful and enter into praising Him.

I will offer to you the sacrifice of thanksgiving and call on the name of the Lord (Psalm 116:17 ESV).

Enter into His gates with thanksgiving, and into His courts with praise. Be thankful to Him, and bless His name. For the Lord is good; His mercy is everlasting, and His truth endures to all generations (Psalm 100:4-5 NKJV).

When life is hard and the times are evil, we especially want to renew our minds to what the will of God is and do it.

Look carefully then how you walk, not as unwise but as wise, making the best use of the time, because the days are evil. Therefore do not be foolish, but understand what the will of the Lord is. And do not get drunk with wine, for that is debauchery, but be filled with the Spirit, addressing one another in psalms and hymns and spiritual songs, singing and making melody to the Lord with your heart, giving thanks always and for everything to God the Father in the name of our Lord Jesus Christ (Ephesians 5:15-20 ESV).

Get a notebook and start writing down the things God has done for you. From being born to saving you from sin, and everything small and large in between, write them down. Put them on paper when you are thankful, so that when you are struggling you can go back and read them as a reminder. Then speak them out, tell others, and rehearse what happened in your mind, remembering the goodness of God toward you.

Behold, it was for my welfare that I had great bitterness; but in love you have delivered my life from the pit of destruction, for you have cast all my sins behind your back. For Sheol does not thank you; death does not praise you; those who go down to the pit do not hope for your faithfulness. The living, the living, he thanks you, as I do this day; the father makes known to the children your faithfulness (Isaiah 38:17-19 ESV).

Proclaiming thanksgiving aloud, and telling all your wondrous deeds (Psalm 26:7 ESV).

Jesus encountered people with needs wherever He went. In Luke 17 we read of ten such men, who had leprosy and needed healing. They all cried out to Him, and He cleansed them; however, only one came back to thank and praise Him. The result was that this man's skin was not only cleansed, but he was made whole.

Now it happened as He went to Jerusalem that He passed through the midst of Samaria and Galilee. Then as He entered a certain village, there met Him ten men who were lepers, who stood afar off. And they lifted up their voices and said, "Jesus, Master, have mercy on us!" So when He saw them, He said to them, "Go, show yourselves to the priests." And so it was that as they went, they were cleansed. And one of them, when he saw that he was healed, returned, and with a loud voice glorified God, and fell down on his face at His feet, giving Him thanks. And he was a Samaritan. So Jesus answered and said, "Were there not ten cleansed? But where are the nine? Were there not any found who returned to give glory to God except this foreigner?" And He said to him, "Arise, go your way. Your faith has made you well" (Luke 17:11-19 NKJV).

Thankfulness can be a powerful weapon against evil, and a potent practice for living a happy and hopeful life.

And so, from the day we heard, we have not ceased to pray for you, asking that you may be filled with the knowledge of his will in all spiritual wisdom and understanding, so as to walk in a manner worthy of the Lord, fully pleasing to him: bearing fruit in every good work and increasing in the knowledge of God; being strengthened with all power, according to his glorious might, for all endurance and patience with joy; giving thanks to the Father, who has qualified you to share in the inheritance of the saints in light. He has delivered us from the domain of darkness and transferred us to the kingdom of his beloved Son, in whom we have redemption, the forgiveness of sins (Colossians 1:9-14 ESV).

Think the Word of God

Reading and contemplating the words of the Bible helps the mind of man.

The unfolding of your words gives light; it gives understanding to the simple (Psalm 119:130 NIV).

In these days, we need understanding. People are searching for answers, for help, and for truth.

Sanctify them by the truth; your Word is truth (John 17:17 NIV).

To sanctify someone or something is to set that person or thing apart for the use intended by its designer[18]. Isn't that what most of us are wanting in our lives—to live and serve the Lord in the way that He has called us to and designed us for? The truth from the Word of God will help us to do that. To spend time in the Word of God not only helps you to know God more deeply and intimately, but also helps you to know yourself. He will reveal truths to you that are specific for you, that you need in order to be your best and to love God.

I wrote in Chapter 2 about a car accident I was in when I was a teenager in high school. One underlying thought that I carried for a long time was, "Why didn't You protect me?" I knew Hebrews 13:5b (ESV), For He has said, *"I will never leave you nor forsake you."* After seeing the smashed car, I knew that was true, but I still had questions. I certainly had prayed and talked to God about it several times, but I did not get an immediate answer. I also knew that Jesus understood what I was feeling and thinking because of Hebrews 4:14-16 (ESV):

Since then we have a great high priest who has passed through the heavens, Jesus, the Son of God, let us hold fast our confession. For we do not have a high priest who is unable to sympathize with our weaknesses, but one who in every respect has been tempted as we are, yet without sin. Let us then with confidence draw near to the throne of grace, that we may receive mercy and find grace to help in time of need.

This truth gave me some comfort—knowing that Jesus, who was intimate with His Father at levels I could not comprehend, was also tempted with feeling, "Where was God?" On the cross before Jesus died, He spoke these words, "My God, my God, why have you forsaken me?" If the one who said He only did what He saw and heard His Father do couldn't see or hear Him at this point in His life, then I knew He understood. I also knew Jesus didn't sin when He felt this way, so I asked Him to help me not to sin in my struggle. I thanked God for saving my life in the accident, but also asked Him if one day He would show me what had happened. Time went by, but He answered my request.

One day when I was lying down, listening to quiet worship music with my eyes closed, I had a vision. It was like I was back in the car at the time of the accident, but everything was happening in slow motion. I turned my head and saw the other car as it hit us. I was sitting in the front seat and was thrown forward, smashing my face into the dash. However, an angel had both its hands on my face. Doctors were always amazed because I had broken my jaw in three places but never had any cuts, or even bruises, on my face, so there were never any signs of harm on the outside. I also saw two angels inside the car, holding the front and back side doors of the car so they didn't smash in on any of us while we were inside. That entire side of the car was later pushed in to half its width, but not until we all were out. There was another angel with its arms around my waist, and a few more attending to my friends. The vision ended, and I cried out to the Lord, "Thank you, thank you, thank you!"

God really was there for me and sent help when I needed Him! I just didn't perceive it, feel it, or see it. Jesus really did understand. He went through it too, and yet, the Father was with us when we needed Him most. "I will never leave you or forsake you" really is true! Our God is faithful, even when I perceive it differently. The words in the song "Waymaker" by Michael W. Smith say just that:

Even when I don't see it, You're working.
Even when I don't feel it, You're working.
You never stop, You never stop working.
You never stop, You never stop working.[19]

This understanding of truth versus my perception has helped me so much in my life. When the circumstances don't seem to fit what I think about God, instead of abandoning Him in my mind, I can go to my Lord who understands and ask for help. Even if I don't get an answer right away, I know He will bring it in due time.

Let us then with confidence draw near to the throne of grace, that we may receive mercy and find grace to help in time of need (Hebrews 4:16 ESV).

This is just one incident in my life where my thoughts—my mind—did not line up with the truth of what Scripture says. Circumstances stare us in the face and sometimes seem more real than the biblical truths we may already know, but that is why the renewing of the mind is so important.

This does not negate the things that have happened to you or me. Bad things happen sometimes, but I don't want them to cause me to sin. I have to choose not to live in and continue to dwell on a perspective that does not agree with what God says. Yes, even when I don't understand. That's when I run to my Savior. Someone once told me to just "put it on the shelf," admitting you don't know and asking God to show you in His good way and timing. I did that with this incident in my life and though it took years, God revealed to me the truth, and I have been set free.

For the mind set on the flesh is death, but the mind set on the Spirit is life and peace (Romans 8:6 NASB).

Jesus was tempted in all ways like us. He gets it! He understands how hard it is, how impossible it seems, how you're feeling, how you're thinking; and He's there to help you. Ask Him. Open up to Him. He can be trusted. He will come to you.

Philippians 2 says that Jesus was made in the likeness of men, and He humbled himself and obeyed, even to the cross. We also need to humble ourselves and obey when circumstances are hard, when we don't understand, when it doesn't seem right or just. This life on earth is not what God originally intended, and it is not what it will become in the future, either; but we can use our minds and thoughts for His purposes and live like Jesus even now. However, that may take doing an inventory of your thoughts and attitudes.

Questions are often used to help evaluate something. They can be the beginning of a thought process to look at what you are thinking. Whenever I tutor students, I use a lot of questions to understand what and how they are thinking. This process helps both me and them to see if their thinking is lining up with the topic we are focusing on. The same works for you. Ask questions of yourself. Do the work that is necessary to consider whether what you are thinking is the mind of Christ—does it line up with Scripture, is it life-giving, does it bring glory to God? Then repent for areas that don't, and humbly ask God to help you think like Jesus. We can be like Him, but it takes deliberate attention and discipline to choose the lifestyle of godly thinking and actions. However, we can do it, and He will help.

A wicked man puts on a bold face, but the upright gives thought to his ways (Proverbs 21:29 ESV).

Fulfil ye my joy, that ye be likeminded, having the same love, being of one accord, of one mind. Let nothing be done through strife or vainglory; but in lowliness of mind let each esteem other better than themselves. Look not every man on his own things, but every man also on the things of others.

Let this mind be in you, which was also in Christ Jesus: who, being in the form of God, thought it not robbery to be equal with God: but made himself of no reputation, and took upon him the form of a servant, and was made in the likeness of men: and being found in fashion as a man, he humbled himself, and became obedient unto death, even the death of the cross. Wherefore God also hath highly exalted him, and given him a name which is above every name: that at the name of Jesus every knee should bow, of things in heaven, and things in earth, and things under the earth; and that every tongue should confess that Jesus Christ is Lord, to the glory of God the Father.

Wherefore, my beloved, as ye have always obeyed, not as in my presence only, but now much more in my absence, work out your own salvation with fear and trembling. For it is God which worketh in you both to will and to do of his good pleasure. Do all things without murmurings and disputings: that ye may be blameless and harmless, the sons of God, without rebuke, in the midst of a crooked and perverse nation, among whom ye shine as lights in the world; holding forth the word of life (Philippians 2:2-16 KJV).

Yes, let the mind of Christ Jesus be in us. Then we can utilize our minds to love God, ourselves, and others day to day.

The Word of God has instructions on what we are and what we are not to think about, meditate on, and ponder. This would be the optimum way to utilize our minds. Let's look at some of that wisdom.

1 Corinthians 13:5b (NKJV) instructs us that the love of God thinks no evil.

Not that we are sufficient of ourselves to think of anything as being from ourselves, but our sufficiency is from God (2 Corinthians 3:5 NKJV).

Brethren, I do not count myself to have apprehended; but one thing I do, forgetting those things which are behind and reaching forward to those things which are ahead, I press toward the goal for the prize of the upward call of God in Christ Jesus. Therefore let us, as many as are mature, have this mind; and if in anything you think otherwise, God will reveal even this to you (Philippians 3:13-15 NKJV).

God will show you when your thinking is not aligned with His. Pay attention when He does.

The end of all things is near. Therefore be alert and of sober mind so that you may pray (1 Peter 4:7 NIV).

One of the things we are not to do with our minds is to pass judgment on others. God is the righteous judge, not us. We are to love one another.

Therefore let us stop passing judgment on one another. Instead, make up your mind not to put any stumbling block or obstacle in the way of a brother or sister (Romans 14:13 NIV).

God instructs us instead to think on things in certain categories, listed in this verse in Philippians.

Finally, brethren, whatsoever things are true, whatsoever things are honest, whatsoever things are just, whatsoever things are pure, whatsoever things are lovely, whatsoever things are of good report; if there be any virtue, and if there be any praise, think on these things (Philippians 4:8 KJV).

Does the majority of your thinking line up with thoughts that are true, honest, just, pure, lovely, of good report, of virtue, and worthy of praise? If not, what can you do to improve your thinking patterns? Doing nothing is not a solution. Attempt to set up a system of checking your thoughts. Setting an alarm on your phone every hour, and doing a mental inventory of what your thoughts were for that hour, is a good starting point. Writing a list of thoughts that are specific to you and your life that fall into the categories in Philippians 4:8, and reading them aloud every day, is another good place to begin. There are plenty of other approaches, some mentioned in the Bible.

Fix these words of mine in your hearts and minds; tie them as symbols on your hands and bind them on your foreheads. Teach them to your children, talking about them when you sit at home and when you walk along the road, when you lie down and when you get up. Write them on the doorframes of your houses and on your gates, so that your days and the days of your children may be many in the land the Lord swore to give your ancestors, as many as the days that the heavens are above the earth. If you carefully observe all these commands I am giving you to follow—to love the Lord your God, to walk in obedience to him and to hold fast to him— then the Lord will drive out all these nations before you, and you will dispossess nations larger and stronger than you. Every place where you set your foot will be yours (Deuteronomy 11:18-24 NIV).

Let the word of Christ dwell in you richly, teaching and admonishing one another in all wisdom, singing psalms and hymns and spiritual songs, with thankfulness in your hearts to God (Colossians 3:16 ESV).

When you read your favorite Bible story, let your mind's eye see it. Let the Scriptures become more alive to you in this way. The people and situations in the Bible really did happen! God created us with an imagination to use for His purposes. Imagine the encounter you are reading about in the Bible, think about it, and your heart may burn within you as it did for the men on the road listening to the resurrected Jesus.

They said to each other, "Did not our hearts burn within us while he talked to us on the road, while he opened to us the Scriptures?" (Luke 24:32 ESV).

One habit I have started is that whenever I catch myself thinking negatively, I then have to think three positive thoughts to replace what I was thinking. This has helped me to change my attitudes and opinions, because I have to look for the good in things instead of focusing on what I don't like.

Find what works for you, but get started in the process of renewing your mind. Arrange your priorities to spend time with God, focusing your thoughts on things that are true, pure, and of good report. Read and study the Word of God so you know its truths. Then base your decisions on them and do what is right. Think what you can be thankful for. Lift your thoughts and words of admiration and love to Him. You will be glad you did.

You will then be loving God with all your mind.

CHAPTER 5

Love God with ALL YOUR STRENGTH

God longs for your strength. Loving God with your strength is the outward expression of what's inside of you. Loving Him is not only with your emotions, your personality, and your thoughts, but with your actions, your time, your resources, and your talents. You demonstrate your love by what you do; that's loving Him with your strength.

One definition of strength is ability, might, and force,[20] so many of us think of strength as bodily or muscular power, but that is not the only type of strength there is. You do not have to be physically strong to show strength. Imagine a little boy watching his mother get screamed at and hit by a boyfriend who then heads out the door. The young child goes over to his mom, puts his arms around her, and says, "It's okay, Mommy. He's not nice. We will be okay without him." That little boy has exemplified strength to his mom, which might help her to make a good choice for herself and her child.

Imagine a man who has had cerebral palsy his whole life. From his bed each morning, he grabs his two walking canes and leans on them to literally drag himself out of bed. His feet flop to the ground as he then takes a belabored step to roll a wheelchair close and slowly climbs in. This is only his first step, besides getting dressed, making his breakfast, getting out the door, and going to work five days a week. This kind of strength, day in and day out, is something I have never had to deal with, but respect immensely.

On the day I called, you answered me; my strength of soul you increased (Psalm 138:3 ESV).

Imagine a parent with a child, diagnosed with cancer at the age of four, who now is twelve years old. The strength this parent faithfully shows through the endless doctor visits and hospital stays, as well as chemo or radiation therapy, is amazing. All so the child will stay hopeful and not be afraid. This strength for another, while her heart is aching, is sacrificial love we all can learn from and admire.

These examples are just a few situations where people demonstrate inner strength by their actions and behavior. All of us have some kind of strength, but we might not always feel strong. There may not always be someone around to help strengthen us when we need it, but we always have the Lord, who comes alongside to lift us up. Even when circumstances seem bleak, He empowers us with what we need at the time.

He gives power to the faint, and to him who has no might he increases strength (Isaiah 40:29 ESV).

May the Lord give strength to his people! May the Lord bless his people with peace! (Psalm 29:11 ESV).

Our God does not leave His people to handle life alone. He is always with us and in us, so we can have the strength we need to move forward in His wisdom and power by way of the Holy Spirit.

Have I not commanded you? Be strong and courageous. Do not be frightened, and do not be dismayed, for the Lord your God is with you wherever you go (Joshua 1:9 ESV).

Self

To be strong doesn't come without effort. Whether physically, mentally, or emotionally, getting strong seems like I have to do something. Do you feel the same way? Self-help, self-effort—self, self, self—is getting a lot of attention these days. Honestly, it can wear you out just thinking about it. Not that I want to just lie around on the couch all day watching the latest series or movies, but once in a while, that can be refreshing. I'm not talking about doing nothing, but I'm also not talking about doing everything! What is the balance?

Yes, we know that faith without works is dead. We know that we must be the ones to "go," but what is the balance between our efforts and God's? How do we rely on God's strength? When I read this verse about David, I usually think that I would like to ask David, "How?" *David strengthened himself in the Lord his God* (1 Samuel 30:6b ESV). He took action by strengthening himself, but you'll notice he did the strengthening in the Lord his God. So, what does that combination of me and Him look like? How, Lord, how?

You can be strengthened by expecting Him to renew you. The expecting is my part; the renewing is His.

But they who wait for the Lord shall renew their strength; they shall mount up with wings like eagles; they shall run and not be weary; they shall walk and not faint (Isaiah 40:31 ESV).

The Wycliffe Bible translation of Isaiah 40:31 states that they who wait expectantly on the Lord shall change their power! As you look to the Lord, expecting Him to come through for you, even though you may not know when or how, your power will be renewed or even changed. Yes, changed from your own power to the power of God within you! That's a promise I hold on to. I expect God to come through for me, to strengthen me, so I can keep going. *Blessed are those whose strength is in you... They go from strength to strength* (Psalm 84:5a,7a ESV).

There are many things we can all accomplish in this life, but we will be more blessed if we allow God to empower us, and do it in His strength and faith. Jeremiah 17:5 (ESV) says, *Thus says the Lord: "Cursed is the man who trusts in man and makes flesh his strength, whose heart turns away from the Lord."* There are no blessings in that. Thinking you have to do everything in your own strength is foolish. Your weakness will eventually show up. You will come to the end of yourself. That's when there's something you can do—cry out to Him, and He increases strength to you.

Have you not known? Have you not heard? The Lord is the everlasting God, the Creator of the ends of the earth. He does not faint or grow weary; his understanding is unsearchable. He gives power to the faint, and to him who has no might he increases strength (Isaiah 40:28-29 ESV).

You can do all things, but it is through Him, because He strengthens you (Philippians 4:13). He is the source. Don't put your trust in yourself—"Me" trust. Put your trust in God—"Him" trust. Then you will prevail over your circumstances.

In the New Testament book of Acts, we see that the apostle Paul certainly demonstrated strength in his life. He was first a Pharisee of Pharisees, having Christians imprisoned and killed. Later, he was converted by Jesus Himself and traveled to reach people with the good news of the kingdom of God. He was stoned, shipwrecked, imprisoned, and eventually killed for His faith. He actually wrote some of the church epistles—Ephesians, Philippians, and Colossians—while in captivity. Listen to some of his words:

A thorn was given me in the flesh, a messenger of Satan to harass me, to keep me from becoming conceited. Three times I pleaded with the Lord about this, that it should leave me. But he said to me, "My grace is sufficient for you, for my power is made perfect in weakness." Therefore I will boast all the more gladly of my weaknesses, so that the power of Christ may rest upon me. For the sake of Christ, then, I am content with weaknesses, insults, hardships, persecutions, and calamities. For when I am weak, then I am strong (2 Corinthians 12:7–10 ESV).

Paul went to the Lord, who encouraged him in his weakness and helped change his perspective.

But we have this treasure in jars of clay, to show that the surpassing power belongs to God and not to us. We are afflicted in every way, but not crushed; perplexed, but not driven to despair; persecuted, but not forsaken; struck down, but not destroyed... we do not lose heart. Though our outer self is wasting away, our inner self is being renewed day by day. For this light momentary affliction is preparing for us an eternal weight of glory beyond all comparison, as we look not to the things that are seen but to the things that are unseen. For the things that are seen are transient, but the things that are unseen are eternal (2 Corinthians 4:7-9,16-18 ESV).

In difficult times, both outwardly and inwardly, the apostle Paul learned to cry out to the Lord, be content no matter what, have a heavenly perspective, and let Christ strengthen him.

Not that I am speaking of being in need, for I have learned in whatever situation I am to be content. I know how to be brought low, and I know how to abound. In any and every circumstance, I have learned the secret of facing plenty and hunger, abundance and need. I can do all things through him who strengthens me (Philippians 4:11-13 ESV).

Certainly, Paul was very aware of his limited situation; however, his focus was not on that alone. He received strength from God to continue his mission of reaching others with the good news of Jesus Christ, whether he was free or bound. Then he looked to how God was using it for good and encouraged others to do the same.

I want you to know, brothers, that what has happened to me has really served to advance the gospel, so that it has become known throughout the whole imperial guard and to all the rest that my imprisonment is for Christ. And most of the brothers, having become confident in the Lord by my imprisonment, are much more bold to speak the word without fear (Philippians 1:12-14 ESV).

His strength was in Christ. Therefore, he continued to carry on with reaching the lost and encouraging the believers by praying, writing letters, and staying faithful to God. All of this he did, even while in lockdown. He had very few connections with people face-to-face while in prison, and obviously none through social media, but his life was about loving and serving the Lord no matter what. Paul demonstrated how to love God with His strength, regardless of his circumstances, even unto death—and so can we.

Remember Jesus Christ, risen from the dead, the offspring of David, as preached in my gospel, for which I am suffering, bound with chains as a criminal. But the word of God is not bound! Therefore I endure everything for the sake of the elect, that they also may obtain the salvation that is in Christ Jesus with eternal glory. The saying is trustworthy, for:

If we have died with him, we will also live with him;

if we endure, we will also reign with him;

if we deny him, he also will deny us;

if we are faithless, he remains faithful— for he cannot deny himself (2 Timothy 2:8-16 ESV).

We can stay strong in the Lord during hard times by relying on His strength, not ours.

Service

One area of loving God with our strength is through service. If our love does not show up in acts that help another, then how deep is our love? If my husband just told me that he loved me, but that's where it ended, I would believe he had feelings of love toward me, but the relationship would not go very deep or be very fulfilling to me. I would want some kind of demonstration of those words. Acts of service, especially when I am in need, would be one way of showing his love.

1 John 3:18 (ESV) says just that: *Little children, let us not love in word or talk but in deed and in truth.*

But be doers of the word, and not hearers only, deceiving yourselves (James 1:22 ESV).

A friend started a ministry to feed the poor, with one of his locations as a drive-through. Another one mentors young men that need father figures in their lives. A nurse friend has a ministry that brings the terminally ill into a home environment for care, while another one opened a home for women in crisis. These are some examples of loving God through serving people in need.

What does it profit, my brethren, if someone says he has faith but does not have works? Can faith save him? If a brother or sister is naked and destitute of daily food, and one of you says to them, "Depart in peace, be warmed and filled," but you do not give them the things which are needed for the body, what does it profit? Thus also faith by itself, if it does not have works, is dead (James 2:14-17 NKJV).

God says whenever we have an opportunity to serve others, do it—especially to those in His family.

Therefore, as we have opportunity, let us do good to all, especially to those who are of the household of faith (Galatians 6:10 NKJV).

This kind of love should also show up in our own homes. We definitely see this with parents loving their children. The care of providing for them, instructing and guiding them, and taking them places are acts of love. To celebrate their victories, and be there for them in hard times too, are ways of showing them love. No matter how young or old they are, parents display their affections and love for their children by what they do for them. My daughter shared at church once about the love of God and talked about specific times my husband and I had showed up to help her. She said that was an important way that she understood God's love and care for her. It wasn't just the hugs and kisses, but the service that spoke to her as well. Is it any different in all our relationships?

If someone has been consistently there for you during hard times, you would definitely appreciate it and be thankful for them. Thoughts and emotions toward them would grow, and at least a friendship kind of love would develop. I have a good friend who has consistently been there for me through the years. I always know I can go to her, and she will come over any time to help. This is a kind of love that means so much to me.

Jesus talked about this in the story of the good Samaritan. Though the Samaritan didn't even know the man, the acts of compassion he displayed were the example Jesus used about loving another.

And he answered, "You shall love the Lord your God with all your heart and with all your soul and with all your strength and with all your mind, and your neighbor as yourself." And he said to him, "You have answered correctly; do this, and you will live." But he, desiring to justify himself, said to Jesus, "And who is my neighbor?" Jesus replied, "A man was going down from Jerusalem to Jericho, and he fell among robbers, who stripped him and beat him and departed, leaving him half dead. Now by chance a priest was going down that road, and when he saw him he passed by on the other side. So likewise a Levite, when he came to the place and saw him, passed by on the other side. But a Samaritan, as he journeyed, came to where he was, and when he saw him, he had compassion. He went to him and bound up his wounds, pouring on oil and wine. Then he set him on his own animal and brought him to an inn and took care of him. And the next day he took out two denarii and gave them to the innkeeper, saying, 'Take care of him, and whatever more you spend, I will repay you when I come back.' Which of these three, do you think, proved to be a neighbor to the man who fell among the robbers?" He said, "The one who showed him mercy." And Jesus said to him, "You go, and do likewise" (Luke 10:27-37 ESV).

The Samaritan saw a need, had compassion, and did something about it. He even went over and above by telling the innkeeper he would be back to repay any costs incurred while caring for the man. He gave of himself—he gave his time and his resources—and not only when it was convenient for him, but when it was needed, right there, right then. Are you willing to give what you have to help someone in need? Are you willing to drop what you are doing to serve another as an act of love to God?

After his resurrection, Jesus appeared to the disciples and many others. During one of those times, recorded in John 21, Jesus asked Simon Peter three times, "Simon, son of John, do you love me?" I have always loved that even though Peter had denied the Lord during Christ's crucifixion experience, Jesus didn't ask him about that. Instead, He asked him about his love for Him, and Peter confirmed his love three times. Each time, the way Jesus responded to Peter was to tell him to feed or tend His sheep and lambs. Jesus was telling Peter that to love Him is to take care of the people of God, to shepherd the flock. He then concluded that conversation with, "Follow me."

As we love Christ, we will follow Him. For some, like Peter, it is to pastor, teach, and take care of the people of God. For others, it may be to own a business providing jobs and giving money and resources to ministries and missions. Still others may be called to serve by feeding the poor, or visiting the sick or those in prison. Some will be led to help the elderly or to rescue children in distress. Many will serve by taking care of their own family or helping a neighbor or friend. There are so many ways and places to give. Wherever God leads you, those are the ways for you to serve. We all need to do what we are instructed to do in the Word and what we sense the Spirit is inspiring us to do. How is God asking you to serve? That's how we can follow Him. That's how we can love Him with our strength.

Then the King will say to those on his right, "Come, you who are blessed by my Father, inherit the kingdom prepared for you from the foundation of the world. For I was hungry and you gave me food, I was thirsty and you gave me drink, I was a stranger and you welcomed me, I was naked and you clothed me, I was sick and you visited me, I was in prison and you came to me." Then the righteous will answer him, saying, "Lord, when did we see you hungry and feed you, or thirsty and give you drink? And when did we see you a stranger and welcome you, or naked and clothe you? And when did we see you sick or in prison and visit you?" And the King will answer them, "Truly, I say to you, as you did it to one of the least of these my brothers, you did it to me" (Matthew 25:34 ESV).

God is clear throughout Scripture that loving God shows up in serving. Let's look at some of the many verses about serving.

Only be very careful to observe the commandment and the law that Moses the servant of the Lord commanded you, to love the Lord your God, and to walk in all his ways and to keep his commandments and to cling to him and to serve him with all your heart and with all your soul (Joshua 22:5 ESV).

Serve the Lord with gladness; come before His presence with singing (Psalm 100:2 NKJV).

For even the Son of Man came not to be served but to serve, and to give his life as a ransom for many (Mark 10:45 ESV).

For you were called to freedom, brothers. Only do not use your freedom as an opportunity for the flesh, but through love serve one another (Galatians 5:13 ESV).

Pure religion and undefiled before God and the Father is this, To visit the fatherless and widows in their affliction, and to keep himself unspotted from the world (James 1:27 KJV).

No one can serve two masters, for either he will hate the one and love the other, or he will be devoted to the one and despise the other. You cannot serve God and money (Matthew 6:24 ESV).

Do we not see verse after verse of God instructing us to serve? It can help to lighten the load for another and show them the kindness and love of God. However, the service alone may not benefit us if the motivation behind it is not love.

If I give away all I have, and if I deliver up my body to be burned, but have not love, I gain nothing (1 Corinthians 13:3 ESV).

Remember, loving God with your strength is a manifestation of what's on the inside. Acts of service to look good may help another, but will not benefit you.

Take heed that you do not do your charitable deeds before men, to be seen by them. Otherwise you have no reward from your Father in heaven. Therefore, when you do a charitable deed, do not sound a trumpet before you as the hypocrites do in the synagogues and in the streets, that they may have glory from men. Assuredly, I say to you, they have their reward. But when you do a charitable deed, do not let your left hand know what your right hand is doing, that your charitable deed may be in secret; and your Father who sees in secret will Himself reward you openly (Matthew 6:1-4 NKJV).

Fulfilling the great commandment is using our bodies, our strength, our resources, and our works with love through acts of service. That would be loving God.

Time

How each of us spends our time is in the category of the physical realm. It is a way to demonstrate our love for God. How do you spend your time? Do you use your time being with God and on things that are pleasing to Him?

Sometimes my husband asks me if I want to go with him to the hardware store. I can honestly say that's not somewhere I want to go. However, I do want to spend time with him, so I usually go.

It's the same principle with God. Obviously, we will be free of time in eternity. While here on earth, though, there are many demands on our time, so can we include God in whatever we are doing? Do we choose to spend our time where He is calling us? Or is our time spent solely on pleasing ourselves or on what demand is the loudest?

Everything seems to be calling out to us in these times to get our attention. The news, social media, entertainment, work, education, responsibilities, and even shopping have become normal everyday activities that take time. Then add the time we are on our phones, driving, and preparing and eating food. These fill up a large part of our day. Next, add the time to take care of family and spend time with friends, and let's not forget sleep. It almost seems like there's very little—if any—time to add anything else, but this is the wrong way of looking at time.

God shouldn't get what's left over. Yes, we all have necessary activities that we must give time to each day, but let's include time with God as one of them. Just as much as I have to go to work, I have to spend time with God. There's no question that I must shop, prepare food, and eat dinner with my family, but there's also no question that I need to spend some time together with God.

Do you get my point? We make time for what's important or necessary to live. Remember that Jesus said that to love God is the first and greatest thing to do. It's important! We need to think of it as necessary, so that we each will devote part of our time to the Lord, who gave His time and entire life for us.

It's not necessarily the amount of time, but the quality of the time spent that matters. What you do is up to you. What brings you closer to Him? That is part of your unique design, so find things that you enjoy doing to be with Him. My son-in-law loves being active outdoors. Climbing mountains and hiking help him get closer to God. Though I love the outdoors, I would be distracted on the task if I were climbing or hiking. Instead, I connect with God when I sit and observe nature. It's how God made us different.

There are so many ways you can spend time with Him alone. Just thinking about Him is great. Talking with Him about anything on your mind and heart is wonderful. Connecting with Him as you walk or run, or even while driving in the car, might work for you. A little time in the morning or a little time before bed can make a big difference.

Very early in the morning, while it was still dark, Jesus got up, left the house and went off to a solitary place, where he prayed (Mark 1:35 NIV).

I rise before dawn and cry for help; I hope in your words (Psalm 119:147 ESV).

Praying or reading the Bible are excellent focused times with Him.

Strengthen me according to your word! (Psalm 119:28b ESV).

Your word is a lamp to my feet and a light to my path (Psalm 119:105 ESV).

You can also take time to journal, where you quiet yourself from the cares of the world and just write. Write whatever comes to mind. You can look at it again later, sensing if it was from the Spirit or from within yourself. Either way, it is time well spent, either hearing from God or getting to know yourself better. I also take time at least once a week to wait on Him. To sit or lie down and just be still has been healing for me. Sometimes I sense His presence and sometimes I don't, but I am submitting myself to Him undistracted, so He can do whatever He wants.

As I mentioned in Chapter 3 about the soul, time spent praising and worshiping Him is also a wonderful way to keep Him first in your life. Whether you use music or just your thoughts and words, giving Him glory in this way—for any amount of time each day—is always profitable.

I will bless the Lord at all times; his praise shall continually be in my mouth (Psalm 34:1 ESV).

And Jesus answered him, "It is written, 'You shall worship the Lord your God, and him only shall you serve'" (Luke 4:8 ESV).

I suggest trying different times and ways, to see what helps you grow in loving God with your time and strength.

You can also spend time with God and accomplish a task too; just include Him. Ask for His help. Be aware of His presence with you. If He is leading you to do something or go somewhere, obeying His direction means you are doing it together, spending time with Him. That pleases Him and shows that you love Him. Once when I went to the grocery store, I sensed His presence with me. I thought for sure there would be someone in the store that needed to hear about the Lord or needed prayer that day. As I shopped, I kept trying to start conversations with people I encountered, but everyone was unusually in a hurry or not talkative that day. Even in the checkout line, no one wanted to talk. When I got back to my car, I asked the Lord, "Did I miss it? Why was Your presence so strong on me in the store?" He answered, "To shop for your family." I immediately repented, because I was looking for a "spiritual" reason, like witnessing, for His presence to be with me in the store. God did not prioritize things the way I did that day. He wanted to be involved with me while I was shopping for my family, not to separate that from being "spiritual." Shopping was serving my family and the most important thing at the time. He was there for me to do it with His help. God says in His Word that whatever we do, we are to do it as serving Him.

And whatever you do, do it heartily, as to the Lord and not to men, knowing that from the Lord you will receive the reward of the inheritance; for you serve the Lord Christ (Colossians 3:23-24 NKJV).

In this life there will always be things that need to get done, but setting aside a part of your day specifically to focus on God is definitely a wise decision. If you love someone, you spend time with them. It also helps you get to know them better. God wants you to know Him, and the more you find out about Him, the more you'll love Him.

The Almighty One wants to spend time with the one He loves too—and that is you! It's like He's saying, "I want you all to Myself for a while." He's a jealous God, and you are His beloved. Devote some of your time to the One who loves you unconditionally, receiving love from Him. Whatever ways you enjoy spending time with God, do it. Your love for Him will grow exponentially.

Talents

People have skills and abilities that they are good at. These can be called talents. If a person has a specific talent it may seem natural and easy to them, whereas someone else would not understand it or could even struggle to learn it. Talents can usually be recognized or seen in the physical realm, so they are considered a strength to love God with. A worship leader is usually gifted in music—whether it is playing an instrument, singing, or writing songs, he or she utilizes that ability to give God glory, thereby loving Him. My husband is excellent at the building arts, like remodeling people's homes, and has the creativity to know what would look good. He definitely gives God glory for this talent, and that would be an expression of him loving the Lord.

Whatever your talent is, the first thing to do is to discover it. Maybe you already know what it is, but for those who don't: what are you passionate about, interested in, or excited to learn about? Just because it is a talent doesn't mean you can't learn how to be better at it. Many abilities in life have to be learned in order to see that it comes easily to you and that you enjoy it. Seek out what it is that interests you and learn from someone who is already proficient in it. Practice the skill and use it, seeing if it is something you want to pursue further. If so, then look for avenues where you can grow in it, and then where you can be a blessing by using it to help and bless others. Your talents are for you, others, and the kingdom of God. There are so many different talents and abilities, and all of them can be used somewhere, for someone; so enjoy it, and let others enjoy it too.

Jesus told the parable of the talents in Matthew 25:14–29 (ESV):

"For it will be like a man going on a journey, who called his servants and entrusted to them his property. To one he gave five talents, to another two, to another one, to each according to his ability. Then he went away. He who had received the five talents went at once and traded with them, and he made five talents more. So also he who had the two talents made two talents more. But he who had received the one talent went and dug in the ground and hid his master's money. Now after a long time the master of those servants came and settled accounts with them. And he who had received the five talents came forward, bringing five talents more, saying, 'Master, you delivered to me five talents; here, I have made five talents more.' His master said to him, 'Well done, good and faithful servant. You have been faithful over a little; I will set you over much. Enter into the joy of your master.' And he also who had the two talents came forward, saying, 'Master, you delivered to me two talents; here, I have made two talents more.' His master said to him, 'Well done, good and faithful servant. You have been faithful over a little; I will set you over much. Enter into the joy of your master.' He also who had received the one talent came forward, saying, 'Master, I knew you to be a hard man, reaping where you did not sow, and gathering where you

scattered no seed, so I was afraid, and I went and hid your tal-
ent in the ground. Here, you have what is yours.' But his mas-
ter answered him, 'You wicked and slothful servant! You knew
that I reap where I have not sown and gather where I scattered
no seed? Then you ought to have invested my money with the
bankers, and at my coming I should have received what was
my own with interest. So take the talent from him and give it
to him who has the ten talents. For to everyone who has will
more be given, and he will have an abundance. But from the
one who has not, even what he has will be taken away.'"

Jesus wants us to use our talents to bring fruitful-
ness, not to just bury them. By using your talents, you
allow others to experience God in ways they may not
usually see Him. For example, an artist at church drew
a picture of a small hand and a larger hand holding a
lampstand together. This reminded me that Jesus is
helping me to be a light to the world, and that I am not
doing it on my own. What a great visual reminder of
that truth! You really don't know how walking in your
talents could inspire someone else to love God, so just
do it. Discover how you can multiply the blessing of
your talent for others and your good Father.

Also, enjoy the talents in the people around you.
Look for the things that are good in people and encourage them to grow by using them. When the members
of the Body of Christ walk in their God-given talents, it

brings glory to God and helps build the kingdom of God on the earth. Then more will be given back to us, and we all can grow in our love for Him.

As each one has received a gift, minister it to one another, as good stewards of the manifold grace of God (1 Peter 4:10 NKJV).

Obey

For the love of God is this, that we obey his commandments. And his commandments are not burdensome (1 John 5:3 NRSV).

1 John 5:3 says it all when it comes to obeying God. If we love God, then we keep His commandments. The first commandment is to love God with all of our hearts, all of our minds, all of our souls, and all of our strength, so we do that whenever we obey Him.

To those who obey His commands, He gives strength to carry out His will.

For your eyes have seen all the great work of the Lord that he did. You shall therefore keep the whole commandment that I command you today, that you may be strong, and go in and take possession of the land that you are going over to possess, and that you may live long in the land that the Lord swore to your fathers to give to them and to their offspring, a land flowing with milk and honey (Deuteronomy 11:7-9 ESV).

However, to just say you love God, to say you keep His Word, to say all the "right" things, but to not carry out the instructions that God gives us in the Bible—that is not true love for God. Faith without works is dead.

Whoever says "I know him" but does not keep his commandments is a liar, and the truth is not in him, but whoever keeps his word, in him truly the love of God is perfected. By this we may know that we are in him: whoever says he abides in him ought to walk in the same way in which he walked (1 John 2:4-6 ESV).

We have an example in Jesus, who will help us obey.

So Jesus said to them, "When you have lifted up the Son of Man, then you will know that I am he, and that I do nothing on my own authority, but speak just as the Father taught me. And he who sent me is with me. He has not left me alone, for I always do the things that are pleasing to him" (John 8:28-29 ESV).

Even when He was tempted, our Savior relied on God. The enemy will try to tempt us to use our own strength and wisdom, but use the words of God instead, like Jesus did. He spoke the Word as a weapon against the lies of Satan, and Satan had to flee. In the midst of temptation, choose to rely on God and obey His Word, like Jesus.

Then Jesus was led up by the Spirit into the wilderness to be tempted by the devil. And after fasting forty days and forty nights, he was hungry. And the tempter came and said to him, "If you are the Son of God, command these stones to become loaves of bread." But he answered, "It is written, 'Man shall not live by bread alone, but by every word that comes from the mouth of God'" (Matthew 4:1-4 ESV).

If obeying God is not what others around you are doing, then remember what Acts 5:29b (ESV) says: *We must obey God rather than men.* The rewards for obeying God will be great.

Jesus answered him, "If anyone loves me, he will keep my word, and my Father will love him, and we will come to him and make our home with him" (John 14:23 ESV).

If you abide in me, and my words abide in you, ask whatever you wish, and it will be done for you. By this my Father is glorified, that you bear much fruit and so prove to be my disciples (John 15:7-8 ESV).

Knowing His words and obeying them brings blessings on your entire household.

Observe and obey all these words which I command you, that it may go well with you and your children after you forever, when you do what is good and right in the sight of the Lord your God (Deuteronomy 12:28 NKJV).

Many can do what's right when it's easy, or when people are watching. However, a real test of obedience comes when no one even knows, or when there is sacrifice or suffering in order to carry it out. When there is pressure or pleasure to do the unrighteous thing, can you stand strong and choose wisely? If you do, our God is faithful and will bless your obedience to Him.

And when you pray, you shall not be like the hypocrites. For they love to pray standing in the synagogues and on the corners of the streets, that they may be seen by men. Assuredly, I say to you, they have their reward. But you, when you pray, go into your room, and when you have shut your door, pray to your Father who is in the secret place; and your Father who sees in secret will reward you openly (Matthew 6:5-6 NKJV).

You then, my child, be strengthened by the grace that is in Christ Jesus, and what you have heard from me in the presence of many witnesses entrust to faithful men, who will be able to teach others also. Share in suffering as a good soldier of Christ Jesus. No soldier gets entangled in civilian pursuits, since his aim is to please the one who enlisted him. An athlete is not crowned unless he competes according to the rules. It is the hard-working farmer who ought to have the first share of the crops. Think over what I say, for the Lord will give you understanding in everything (2 Timothy 2:1-7 ESV).

For those in countries where being a Christian is against the law, obeying God can be a matter of life and death. It would take great strength to withstand the pressure of torture or the threat of death without breaking down.

God is our refuge and strength, an ever-present help in trouble (Psalm 46:1 NIV).

Your love for God must mean more to you than your own life.

And do not fear those who kill the body but cannot kill the soul. Rather fear him who can destroy both soul and body in hell. Are not two sparrows sold for a penny? And not one of them will fall to the ground apart from your Father. But even the hairs of your head are all numbered. Fear not, therefore; you are of more value than many sparrows. So everyone who acknowledges me before men, I also will acknowledge before my Father who is in heaven, but whoever denies me before men, I also will deny before my Father who is in heaven (Matthew 10:28-33 ESV).

Since the church began, Christians have died for their faith. Throughout the centuries, many have given their lives because they would not deny Him. Could we, in this day and time, do the same? Have the conveniences of our culture weakened our resolve and deceived us into thinking it shouldn't be hard to be a Christian? Jesus said otherwise.

Therefore do not worry about tomorrow, for tomorrow will worry about its own things. Sufficient for the day is its own trouble (Matthew 6:34 NKJV).

These things I have spoken to you, that in Me you may have peace. In the world you will have tribulation; but be of good cheer, I have overcome the world (John 16:33 NKJV).

Be encouraged, my brothers and sisters, for God is always with you.

Fear not, for I am with you; be not dismayed, for I am your God. I will strengthen you, yes, I will help you, I will uphold you with My righteous right hand (Isaiah 41:10 NKJV).

You are of great value to Him, and there will be rewards in heaven for your faithfulness to God, so stand firm.

Therefore take up the whole armor of God, that you may be able to withstand in the evil day, and having done all, to stand (Ephesians 6:13 NKJV).

As the Body of Christ, let's be praying for those persecuted for Him.

Do not fear any of those things which you are about to suffer. Indeed, the devil is about to throw some of you into prison, that you may be tested, and you will have tribulation ten days. Be faithful until death, and I will give you the crown of life. "He who has an ear, let him hear what the Spirit says to the churches. He who overcomes shall not be hurt by the second death" (Revelation 2:10-11 NKJV).

I know your deeds. See, I have placed before you an open door that no one can shut. I know that you have little strength, yet you have kept my word and have not denied my name (Revelation 3:8 NIV).

To submit to Jesus' words in our lives is not always going to be easy or accepted, but the promise of God is that if you do, you will be blessed and favored by God for eternity.

He said, "Blessed rather are those who hear the word of God and keep it!" (Luke 11:28 ESV).

Why do you call me "Lord, Lord," and not do what I tell you? Everyone who comes to me and hears my words and does them, I will show you what he is like: he is like a man building a house, who dug deep and laid the foundation on the rock. And when a flood arose, the stream broke against that house and could not shake it, because it had been well built (Luke 6:46-48 ESV).

Faithfully obey God, showing Him your love in this way, and you will receive a crown in heaven. Remind yourself that eternal rewards are worth the pain and hardships of this life.

Blessed is the man who remains steadfast under trial, for when he has stood the test he will receive the crown of life, which God has promised to those who love him (James 1:12 ESV).

Love God with all your strength.

CHAPTER 6

Love God Completely

God wants all of you.

To love God is the greatest commandment, but it is also the greatest privilege. To love the One who made you, to love the One who saved you, to love the One who is preparing a place for you in heaven, is a joy and an honor. Drawing close to Him to love Him also causes you to experience His love for you in a greater way. Then we will also have all of eternity to continue experiencing the fullness of His love.

The Lord has appeared of old to me, saying: "Yes, I have loved you with an everlasting love; therefore with lovingkindness I have drawn you" (Jeremiah 31:3 NKJV).

He delights over you with great joy. When my grandson Jack comes over to visit, my day is filled with joy, and I want to do things to bless him. God is so much greater than that as He pours out His love on you.

If you then, being evil, know how to give good gifts to your children, how much more will your Father who is in heaven give good things to those who ask Him! (Matthew 7:11 NKJV).

God tells us of His love in His Word, but He knew that wouldn't be enough, so He showed us.

But God shows his love for us in that while we were still sinners, Christ died for us (Romans 5:8 ESV).

God never takes His love away. Nothing we do separates His love from us.

For I am persuaded that neither death nor life, nor angels nor principalities nor powers, nor things present nor things to come, nor height nor depth, nor any other created thing, shall be able to separate us from the love of God which is in Christ Jesus our Lord (Romans 8:38-39 NKJV).

There is nothing in this life that is greater than God's love.

Because Your lovingkindness is better than life, my lips shall praise You (Psalm 63:3 NKJV).

He gave us His all—everything He is, which is all love.

We have known and believed the love that God has for us. God is love, and he who abides in love abides in God, and God in him (1 John 4:16 NKJV).

Love is what you were made for. You were designed to be loved and to love. God wants you to receive the fullness of His love. Then when you do, you can love Him back, and become more like Him. You will start looking like Christ. You will start looking like your heavenly Father.

But we all, with open face beholding as in a glass the glory of the Lord, are changed into the same image from glory to glory, even as by the Spirit of the Lord (2 Corinthians 3:18 KJV).

As you receive God's love and then love Him back, the real you comes alive!

Your heart, your soul, your mind, and your strength are a holy combination that was conceived in heaven by God Himself. The Holy Creator loved you so much that He gave you everything you needed to be the best you can be. As you give yourself to God in love, you begin to experience the fullness of who you are in Christ.

That completeness comes from the oneness in God Himself.

For in Him dwells all the fullness of the Godhead bodily; and you are complete in Him, who is the head of all principality and power (Colossians 2:9-10 NKJV).

You are complete in Him. Therefore, you can grow in each area of heart, soul, mind, and strength, but you love God with all of it in unity.

God did not only give a part of Himself. He gave everything. We can do the same. We give Him all of who we are.

The design of this book is to help us grow into wholeness for God, ourselves, and others, so we can love with all of who He created us to be. As we deal with specific aspects of ourselves, to align them with His wisdom and ways, we will experience more blessings and wholeness. We're not looking for what's wrong with us. We're focusing on the good design of God in us and doing His will to bring healing. Then as healing comes, you and I become free to be real about our emotions, thoughts, personalities, and actions. You become you—the real you, the you God created you to be. Yes, even awesomely and wonderfully made. That's God's heart—to love us to freedom. Then we are free to give, to serve, to interact, and to love out of that liberty with everything we're becoming.

God's intentions are always good. He didn't give us the first commandment to love Him because He was incomplete without our love. He did it for us.

Once, when I was interning with a pastor's wife in her home, I was asked to change the sheets in one of the extra bedrooms upstairs because a guest was coming. She was going to be meeting with someone downstairs, so this would help her out. As I headed to the room, I stopped off in another bedroom to check on a student who was staying there recuperating from a procedure. I wanted to see if she needed anything. I knew the student, so we began talking, laughing, and catching up for longer than I should have. I kept thinking that I needed to go, but I was enjoying the time together, so I didn't pull away. All of a sudden, the pastor's wife was standing behind me. She gently said, "I asked you to do something for me." Apologetically, I went straight to the other bedroom and began working. As I thought about it later, I asked the Lord why she would interrupt her meeting to come upstairs to reprove me. His answer surprised me. "I inspired her to come upstairs. I have blessings that I want to give you, and you would have missed out on them if you weren't obedient." It was then that I realized God's intention is always for my good. He does not punish us, even when we make mistakes. His heart is to bless His people. He reproves us to enlighten us to His will, so that we can receive all the wonderful blessings He has planned for us.

Oh, give thanks to the Lord, for He is good! For His mercy endures forever (Psalm 118:29 NKJV).

This is His intention with the first and great commandment. God asks us to be obedient to love Him because He knows when we do, we will receive the blessings He wants to give us.

That's God's heart. He chose you to be His child and lavished you with His love. He's always working on your behalf.

See what great love the Father has lavished on us, that we should be called children of God! And that is what we are! (1 John 3:1a NIV).

The Son of God hung on the cross so we could become the sons and daughters of God.

Looking unto Jesus, the author and finisher of our faith, who for the joy that was set before Him endured the cross, despising the shame, and has sat down at the right hand of the throne of God (Hebrews 12:2 NKJV).

His joy was for you and me to be set free from the captivity of sin and destruction, which robs us of being our true selves. The redemption that Christ bought back for us through his death and resurrection opens the door for us to connect with the Father, the same way Jesus is connected with Him. We can then experience the love of the Father. We can experience that He is good and kind. Out of that, we can love God and trust Him to receive all that He has for us.

I woke up one morning saying, *"Trust in the Lord with all your heart, with all your soul, with all your mind, and with all your strength." Wait a minute, I thought, that's not what the first commandment says! It says, "LOVE the Lord your God with all your heart and with all your soul and with all your mind and with all your strength."* So why was I thinking about trust in that verse? As I pondered the thought, another verse came to mind:

Trust in the Lord with all your heart (there's the heart), *and lean not on your own understanding* (wait a minute, there's the mind); *in all your ways* (hey, that's the soul) *acknowledge Him, and He shall direct your paths* (which is the strength or physical side) (Proverbs 3:5-6 NKJV).

This was the Holy Spirit, leading me into the truth that love and trust are intimately linked together. To trust someone that you love is vital to your relationship, so much so that if you didn't trust that person, your love would wane. God's love for us has been demonstrated through the life and death of His Son. Jesus could have called out to His Father to send angels to rescue Him from the torture of the cross.

Or do you think that I cannot now pray to My Father, and He will provide Me with more than twelve legions of angels? (Matthew 26:53 NKJV).

He didn't, because He loves us. The Father watched as the Son He loves was beaten, tortured, and crucified, but He didn't stop it, because He loves us. This demonstration of love proves we can trust Him. We have loved people for far less than that. How much more can we love and trust God?

Greater love has no one than this, than to lay down one's life for his friends (John 15:13 NKJV).

God's reliable, limitless love gives us wholeness and eternal life.

But I trust in your unfailing love; my heart rejoices in your salvation (Psalm 13:5 NIV).

Jesus prayed that we would be so filled with God's love that we would become one with them.

That they may all be one, just as you, Father, are in me, and I in you, that they also may be in us, so that the world may believe that you have sent me. The glory that you have given me I have given to them, that they may be one even as we are one, I in them and you in me, that they may become perfectly one, so that the world may know that you sent me and loved them even as you loved me (John 17:21-23 ESV).

We've been given the heart of the Father and the mind of Christ, working through the Spirit in our physical bodies. Wow, we are one! Now we want to grow by walking into the oneness that we've already been given. As our heart, soul, mind, and strength are committed to love Him and walk in His ways, we will. It could look like the way Jesus walked on the earth—His love, His actions, His words, and His miracles.

Most assuredly, I say to you, he who believes in Me, the works that I do he will do also; and greater works than these he will do, because I go to My Father. And whatever you ask in My name, that I will do, that the Father may be glorified in the Son. If you ask anything in My name, I will do it (John 14:12-14 NKJV).

It would show up through the fruit of the Spirit: love, joy, peace, patience, gentleness, goodness, faith, meekness and self-control (Galatians 5:22-23), first in ourselves, and then demonstrated to the world. In this day and time, who doesn't need that? As we submit to God's will and ways for us, we can live in oneness with Him.

There is much joy when we are united in oneness with God. When we hold our love back from Him—knowingly or unknowingly—our intimacy, and therefore our joy, are affected. When we look at the influences on our heart, soul, mind, and strength, it can help us to become aware of areas that may be getting in the way of loving Him. Then we can do something to change it so we can love Him more and receive the blessings that come with it.

Receiving His love and giving Him ours in return is how Christians are designed to live. That kind of joy, peace, and love are life-giving and a great witness to others. Many will want what we have if we shine our light that way.

You are the light of the world. A city that is set on a hill cannot be hidden. Nor do they light a lamp and put it under a basket, but on a lampstand, and it gives light to all who are in the house. Let your light so shine before men, that they may see your good works and glorify your Father in heaven (Matthew 5:14-16 NKJV).

For those who love God, the blessings are many. These are just a few of the promises recorded in the Bible about that.

Know therefore that the Lord your God is God, the faithful God who keeps covenant and steadfast love with those who love him and keep his commandments, to a thousand generations (Deuteronomy 7:9 ESV).

And we know that for those who love God all things work together for good, for those who are called according to His purpose (Romans 8:28 ESV).

But as it is written, Eye hath not seen, nor ear heard, neither have entered into the heart of man, the things which God hath prepared for them that love him (1 Corinthians 2:9 BRG).

Yes, God has promised good things to those who love Him, but the sweetest reward for loving God is getting closer to God Himself.

"Whoever has my commandments and keeps them, he it is who loves me. And he who loves me will be loved by my Father,

and I will love him and manifest myself to him." Judas (not Iscariot) said to him, "Lord, how is it that you will manifest yourself to us, and not to the world?" Jesus answered him, "If anyone loves me, he will keep my word, and my Father will love him, and we will come to him and make our home with him" (John 14:21-23 ESV).

In this life and in the next, loving God brings you close to Him. It will bring you into His presence, to be with Him forever.

In my Father's house are many rooms. If it were not so, would I have told you that I go to prepare a place for you? And if I go and prepare a place for you, I will come again and will take you to myself, that where I am you may be also (John 14:2-3 ESV).

Knowing that he who raised the Lord Jesus will raise us also with Jesus and bring us with you into his presence (2 Corinthians 4:14 ESV).

Is this not the greatest reward for loving God with all that you are?

When Christ who is your life appears, then you also will appear with him in glory (Colossians 3:4 ESV).

And I saw the holy city, new Jerusalem, coming down out of heaven from God, prepared as a bride adorned for her husband. And I heard a loud voice from the throne saying, "Behold, the dwelling place of God is with man. He will dwell with them, and they will be his people, and God himself will be with them as their God. He will wipe away every tear from their eyes, and death shall be no more, neither shall there be mourning, nor crying, nor pain anymore, for the former things have passed away." And he who was seated on the throne said, "Behold, I am making all things new" (Revelation 21:2-5 ESV).

We cannot even know all the glory that we will behold when we are with Him forever, but can we raise our standard of living to focus ahead to heaven, and the glory where we will be with Christ forever? Let the thought of greater things for us there cause us to let go of the temporary hardships of today to praise Him, trust Him, and love Him with all of our lives.

The Christian life is *all about love.*

Without love, everything we believe is a lie. With love, our faith is sure, because *Christ... dwell[s] in your hearts through faith; that you [are] rooted and grounded in love* (Ephesians 3:17 NKJV).

Without love, everything we are falls apart. With love, there's a reason to live, because *in this the love of*

God was made manifest among us, that God sent his only Son into the world, so that we might live through him (1 John 4:9 ESV).

Without love, we are without God. With love, there's hope for the world, because *love bears all things, believes all things, hopes all things, endures all things* (1 Corinthians 13:7 ESV).

Love changes everything.

Without it, human beings were doomed for destruction. With it, we were given eternal life, because *God so loved the world, that he gave his only Son, that whoever believes in him should not perish but have eternal life* (John 3:16 ESV).

Without love, people are lonely, depressed, hopeless, and alone. With love, we have togetherness, hope, vision, and unity, because behold, *how good and how pleasant it is for brethren to dwell together in unity!* (Psalm 133:1 NKJV).

Without love, there is so much sorrow, turmoil, fear, shame, and hate in the world. With love, there is joy, peace, faith, goodness, and kindness in the world, because *the fruit of the Spirit is love, joy, peace, patience, kind-*

ness, goodness, faith, gentleness, and self-control (Galatians 5:22-23a WEB).

Without love, the human race has nowhere to go but down. With love, we have only one way to go—up!

Up to words and works of love and grace.

Now may our Lord Jesus Christ himself, and God our Father, who loved us and gave us eternal comfort and good hope through grace, comfort your hearts and establish them in every good work and word (2 Thessalonians 2:16-17 ESV).

Up to the heavenly places.

Even when we were dead in our trespasses, made us alive together with Christ—by grace you have been saved— and raised us up with him and seated us with him in the heavenly places in Christ Jesus, so that in the coming ages he might show the immeasurable riches of his grace in kindness toward us in Christ Jesus (Ephesians 2:5-7 ESV).

Up to the Father.

See what kind of love the Father has given to us, that we should be called children of God; and so we are (1 John 3:1a ESV).

Up to His glory.

Blessed be his glorious name forever; may the whole earth be filled with his glory! Amen and Amen! (Psalm 72:19 ESV).

To love God with all of our heart—pure, poured out, devoted to Him—will be refreshing to us and those around us. To love Him with all of our soul—walking in hope and in the liberty of being our true selves—will be freeing and will bring glory to God. To love God with all of our mind—being thankful and renewed to His truth—will be amazing and an inspiration to others. To love Him with all of our strength—spending our time, talents, and actions in godly character—will be rewarding and will affect the world around us for Him.

LOVE NEVER FAILS (1 Corinthians 13:8a NKJV).

Pouring out my heart, soul, mind, and strength to Him in love has become the joy and purpose of my life. It is the FIRST thing I want to do and the GREATEST thing I've ever done with my life. Join me in this pursuit to love God as much as possible each day, every day, for the rest of your life. The benefits are beyond description and eternal.

Love God with all of who you are!

About the Author

Elaine Leonard has been a teacher of God's Word for many years through the avenues of Christian school education, children's ministry, church equipping groups and classes, house churches, seminars, and individual mentoring. Her passion is to see the members of the Body of Christ walking in their destinies, equipped to love God well, and demonstrating it in love to others. She is the blessed wife of Larry, mother of three fantastic children, and grandmother to two very adorable grandchildren.

Endnotes

1 "Heart." Def. 1. Cambridge University Press Dictionary, 2020. https://dictionary.cambridge.org/dictionary/english/heart

2 "Heart." Def. 2. Cambridge University Press Dictionary, 2020. https://dictionary.cambridge.org/dictionary/english/heart

3 "Empathy." Def 1. Oxford Dictionary, Lexio.com, 2020. https://www.lexico.com/definition/empathy

4 Mayo Clinic Staff. "Forgiveness: Letting go of grudges and bitterness." Healthy Lifestyle, Adult Health, MFMER, 1998-2020. http://www.mayoclinic.org/healthy-lifestyle/adult-health/in-depth/forgiveness/art-20047692

5 Sick G770." Def. 1. Strong's Concordance, Greek Dictionary, 2017. https://www.quotescosmos.com/bible/bible-concordance/G770.html#:~:text=

6 Sides, Dale. Perfect Redemption. Bedford, Virginia: Liberating Publications, Inc, 2004.

7 "Diligence." Def. 1. Oxford Dictionary. https://www.lexico.com/definition/diligence

8 "Treasure." Oxford Advanced Learning Diction-

ary, Oxford University Press, 2020. https://www.
oxfordlearnersdictionaries.com/us/definition/eng-
lish/treasure_2

9 ”Soul - religion, philosophy.” Encyclopaedia Britannica. Encyclopaedia Britannica, Inc, 2020. https://
www.britannica.com/topic/soul-religion-and-
philosophy#:~:text=

10 "Identity." Def. 1. Collins English Dictionary – Complete and Unabridged, 12th Edition, HarperCollins
Publishers, 2014. https://www.collinsdictionary.
com/dictionary/english/identities

11 "How Animals Adapt." Unbelievably Amazing
Examples of Animal Adaptations. Buzzle.com, Inc.
https://animalsake.com/animal-adaptations

12 Taylor, Paul S., "Did Jesus really sweat drops
of blood?" Christian Answers Network Website
(Marysville, WA: Films for Christ, 2002). https://
christiananswers.net/q-eden/edn-t018.html

13 "Hope." Entry 1 transitive verb. Merriam-Webster
Dictionary. https://www.merriam-webster.com/
dictionary/hope#:~:text=

14 "Mind." Def. 1. The Compact Oxford English Dictionary, Oxford University Press, 1991.

15 Burlamaqui, Jean Jacques, "Of the rights of ambassadors," The Principles of Natural and Politic Law
(1748), Lonang Institute, 2020. https://lonang.com/
library/reference/burlamaqui-natural-politic-law/
burl-2415/#:~:text=

16 "I Will Fear No More" by The Afters.

17 Harvard Health Publishing, Harvard Mental Health

Letter. "In Praise of Gratitude," updated June 5, 2019. Published November 2011. https://www.health.harvard.edu/mind-and-mood/in-praise-of-gratitude

18 "Sanctification." Baker's Evangelical Dictionary of Biblical Theology. Copyright © 1996 by Walter A. Elwell. Baker Books, division of Baker Book House Company, Grand Rapids, Michigan USA. Salem Web Network, Bible Study Tools, 2020. https://www.biblestudytools.com/dictionaries/bakers-evangelical-dictionary/sanctification.html

19 "Waymaker" by Michael W. Smith.

20 "Strength 2479." Strong's Exhaustive Concordance, Biblehub.com. https://biblehub.com/greek/2479.htm

Abbreviations of the Bible Translations used:

BRG – Blue, Red, Gold Letter Edition
CEB – Common English Bible
CSB – Christian Standard Bible
ESV – English Standard Version
KJV – King James Version
NASB – New American Standard Bible
NCV – New Century Version
NIV – New International Version
NKJV – New King James Version
NRSV – New Revised Standard Version
TLB – The Living Bible
WEB – World English Bible

CPSIA information can be obtained
at www.ICGtesting.com
Printed in the USA
FSHW020314280121
78087FS